A Slice
of
Humboldt Pie
Stories & Recipes

by Natasha Wing

D1738752

Wing Books
Arcata, California

Wing Books
75 Sunkist Lane
Arcata, CA 95519-9274

For information about purchasing books,
use order form at back or
contact Natasha Wing at (707) 825-7575

Written and designed by Natasha Wing

Manufactured in the United States of America

ISBN 0-9758719-0-0

2 3 4 5 6 7 8 9 10

The author acknowledges permission to reprint the following
material:
cover photo by Barrie Love
pg. 9 "Hazel Jackson"
p. 18 "Marge Taylor" photographed by Barrie Love
p. 159 recipe from Toni's #1 restaurant
p. 169 recipe from "Huckleberries and Crabmeat: Recipes from
the Pacific Coast" by Carol Cate

Printed in the United States by Morris Publishing
3212 East Highway 30
Kearney, NE 68847
1-800-650-7888

To all the pie bakers in Humboldt County who allowed me into their homes, and shared their stories and pies with me.

Thanks to my official pie tasters: my sweet-toothed husband, Dan Wing, and Barrie and Wade Love.

Stories

Recipes

More Recipes

A favorite filling may be the excuse to eat pie, but it should be the crust that makes the occasion memorable.

Bernard Clayton, Jr., The Complete Book of Pastry Sweet & Savory

When you're a writer, people always want to know where you get your ideas, so I figure I've got some explaining to do.

My friend, June the gardener, loaned me "American Pie: Slices of Life (and Pie) from America's Back Roads" by Pascale Le Draoulec.

"It's really good, the way she writes about the people she meets when she's looking for pie," said June.

June wanted to share a good story with me. What she really did was plant a seed - for another book on pies.

I am a pie baker, although lately my crusts have been giving me trouble. They are tough and don't roll out well. When I pick up the dough to place it in the pie plate, it cracks. So as much as I love the flavor of pies, I've been avoiding making them because of Fear of Crust Failure.

Luckily, my husband prefers taste over looks.

Yet I wanted both.

I decided to take a slice of Le Draoulec's "American Pie" and interview pie makers in Humboldt County to see if their secrets - whether they be Crisco versus oil, vinegar or a pinch of sugar, or ice cold versus tap water - could help me in my quest for the perfect crust.

I discovered much more than great recipes - I met wonderful people who invited me into their homes and businesses to talk over slices of homemade pie. I learned of new resources for both native fruits and locally farmed fruits. But most of all, I developed a new appreciation for Humboldt County.

May your pie-eating occasions be as memorable as mine were. And may they be shared with friends - old and new.

The Mommy Myth

Dan's mom, the legendary pie baker.

Looking forward to a future together.

Dan and I were married in Arizona, and two weeks later, we were heading to Humboldt County in a U-Haul. Dan had taken a job with Caltrans.

As a displaced newlywed, I was faced with lots of challenges - adjusting to married life, finding a job, making friends, and cooking.

My cooking skills were marginal, relying mostly on steaming and boiling, so I prayed my baking would more than make up for my culinary shortcomings.

I was really good at making banana bread and cookies, but Dan hoped he had married someone who could bake a pie as good as his mom's. Although his mother was deceased long before we married, her pies still held a spell over him. If it was true that the way to a man's heart was through his stomach, I had to break his mom's spell and cast a new one.

I don't even remember the flavor of the first pie I made for Dan, but I do remember nervously serving him a slice, then silently waiting for the verdict. When he declared that it was as good as his mom's, I think every cell in my body breathed a collective sigh of relief.

Fifteen years later, upon talking to his oldest sister, Carol, I asked if their mother did anything special to her pies.

"Oh, no. Mother just used water, shortening, salt and flour for her crusts."

So that was it. They were just regular pies.

But what made them special to Dan was that they were made by the woman he loved most in the world - his mother. And now that he had a new woman in his life he loved, my pies were just as delicious.

My sister-in-law, Carol, discovered a better crust recipe than her mom's after making 70 pies one Thanksgiving for the homeless through her church. She says it makes the crust flakier and it rolls out better.

Vinegar 3-Pie Crust

Makes three 8" pie crusts

3 c. flour
1-1/2 c. shortening
1 tsp. salt
1/3 c. cold water
1 T. vinegar
1 egg

Mix flour, salt and shortening until crumbly. In another bowl mix water, egg and vinegar. Add to flour mixture. Make into 3 balls. Chill overnight. Roll out into 8" crusts.

Note: Keeps for 1 week in freezer. Thaw out before rolling.

Dan's Dad's favorite pie that Dan's Mom made was Butterscotch Pie.

Butterscotch Pie

One baked 9" single pie crust

1 c. brown sugar
3 T. cornstarch
1-1/2 c. milk
1 c. water
3 egg yolks
1 tsp. vanilla
1/3 c. butter

In saucepan, mix sugar and cornstarch. Pour in milk and water gradually and cook over low to medium heat, stirring constantly until it boils (more like when it erupts in a big bubble like a volcano). Cook for one minute then take off heat. Beat egg yolks separately in another bowl. Stir in half of the hot mixture with the eggs and blend. Then pour this back into saucepan. Cook another minute. Remove from heat and put in vanilla and butter. Stir, then pour in baked pie shell. Cool. Serve with whipped cream. Refrigerate remaining pie.

"Pie aren't squared, pie are round."

L.P., Dan's dad

That Voodoo Magic

Hazel Jackson delivers a pie during the Depresssion.

Humboldt County has served as the back-drop to several movies including "Outbreak," "The Lost World" and "The Majestic."

I met Barrie Love on the set of "The Majestic" when we were both extras in the movie filmed in the Victorian Village of Ferndale. She was one of the lucky ones who got to use her own natural blond hair while the rest of us suffered in wigs that made our scalps itch. Besides having a cool, bluesy stage name - Barrie Love - she has an infectious adventurous spirit and a great laugh to match. We've been good pals ever since, being able to talk about everything from tarot cards to lip lifts.

She waved her arms about while we walked through the red-wood forest in Arcata. "Making pie crusts is like voodoo. There's flour, there's Crisco, and then magically there's a crust!"

"What's so intimidating about flour, Crisco, salt and water?" I asked.

"I'm afraid if it doesn't come out there'll be this feeling of doom, so I just buy frozen ones. I know I'll never be able to make a crust like my gramma's so why try."

She shrugged it off with an "oh well" laugh. But there it was hanging between us. The Ghost of Gramma and all she represented to Barrie as the standard in pie making.

Barrie's grandmother, Hazel Jackson, was from the time when women wore pearls, heels and dresses around the house. Even while they vacuumed.

One day during the Depression, Hazel's husband was laid off from his job as a foreman at a tool and die plant. He told Hazel he was going to look for a job and never came back. He left her with four children to raise, and house payments.

After losing the house, Hazel moved to her parents' farm in Waverly, Iowa. Her oldest child got a job in town. Her 11 year old son, Wendell, went to her brother's farm to work while Hazel cared for the two youngest. But having her kids split up was more than she could bear.

She moved the family into town and opened a pie shop in the front of the house. She sent the boys out on their bikes with samples. People couldn't resist her fabulous pies! The kids came back with orders from neighbors and restaurants, and Hazel baked and baked until they were filled. The pies helped keep her family afloat during the Depression.

In the 1950s, after the youngest was grown and out of the house, Hazel moved to California. Baby Barrie came along in 1959.

Barrie started watching her grandmother bake pies when she was about four years old.

"I remember standing on a chair because I was so little watching my gramma make pies. Her kitchen was old and dark from bad lighting, which seemed to add to all the mystery of baking." That voodoo thing again.

"Sometimes now I get cravings for a slice of pie in the afternoon because my gramma and I would do that. She'd have hers with coffee, and I'd have mine with milk."

After we got back from our walk, Barrie showed me a hand-tinted photo of her grandmother she had hanging in her kitchen. Hazel had a pie in her hand on her way to deliver it to a neighbor. I was in awe of this woman who took a bad situation and turned it around with pies.

To pay tribute to Hazel, I wanted to include a recipe for rhubarb pie since that was the one of her grandmother's Barrie remembered most fondly. But in speaking with Hazel's daughter-in-law, Patsy Jackson (Barrie's mom), I learned that Hazel didn't write down her pie recipes.

"She just threw things in and everything turned out wonderfully," said Patsy, batting her long lashes in wonderment. "I never knew how to make her pie crust - she did a pinch of this, a pinch of that and whipped one up. They always came out real flaky. I do know she used Crisco."

Hazel was the only person she knew who could wear a black silk suit and never get a speck of flour on her.

Patsy laughed thinking about the first time she tried to make a pie for her new husband, Wendell. She didn't get past the crust.

"It stuck to the board and came up in pieces. When I tried to fix it, it turned all grey for some reason. I was so mad that I rolled it up in a ball and threw it from the kitchen into our bedroom and just forgot about it. My husband came home and went to change his clothes. He called out, 'What's this funny grey thing in here?' I don't want to talk about it! I shouted back."

Patsy paused. "I'll make all other kinds of desserts, but not pie. Mine would never be as good as my mother-in-law's."

A few days later, Barrie called.

"Guess what. My mom talked to my sister Kendell and she has gramma's pie crust recipe."

"Oh, great!"

"There's this part about cutting the Crisco with two knives. What's that all about?"

"You've got to take the knives and chop, chop, chop at the shortening to make it into little crumbs. I used to do that until I got a pastry blender."

"It's a mystery to me," said Barrie.

"Did your sister get your grandma's recipe for rhubarb pie?"

Turns out she didn't have that. After some more searching through recipe boxes and books, no one in the family turned up a recipe for gramma's rhubarb pie. But Patsy did find this very interesting cook book with recipes from the White House. Its muted white cover had a brown burn mark where it must have been too close to a stove burner once.

"The Presidential Cook Book" was printed in 1907 as an adaptation of the "White House Cook Book." According to the publisher's preface, this peasant form was "more easily in the reach of the masses in point of price" and "fills the requirements of housekeepers of all classes."

I perused through the yellowed pages and came upon some interesting tips for pie making. On page 285 under "HOW TO MAKE A PIE" it read:

"After making the crust, take a portion of it, roll it out and fit it into a buttered pie-plate by cutting it off evenly around the edge;

gather up the scraps left from cutting and make into another sheet for the top crust; roll it a little thinner than the under crust; lap one half over the other and cut three or four slits about a quarter of an inch from the folded edge, (this prevents the steam from escaping through the rim of the pie, and causing the juices to run out from the edges.)"

Obviously the White House wasn't equipped with rollout cloths with preprinted 8", 9", and 10" circles. Yet I had never heard of rolling the top layer thinner than the bottom layer. That was a good tip. And buttering the pie plate. I'd have to try that.

There was even a little tip about what to do with leftover crust. "Roll it thin, cut it in small squares and bake. Just before tea, put a spoonful of raspberry jelly on each square."

Great idea!

The section continued:

"Now fill your pie-plate with your prepared filling, wet the top edge of the rim, lay the upper crust across the centre of the pie, turn back the half that is lapped over, seal the two edges together by slightly pressing down with your thumb, then notch evenly and regularly with a three-tined fork, dipping occasionally in flour to prevent sticking. Bake in a rather quick oven a light brown, and until the filling boils up through the slits in the upper crust.

"To prevent the juice soaking through the crust, making it soggy, wet the under crust with the white of an egg, just before you put in the pie mixture. If the top of the pie is brushed over with the egg, it gives it a beautiful glaze."

A pie fit for the president is fit for us regular folks too. So I flipped through the pages to see if there was a recipe for rhubarb pie. Among the recipes for Apple and Peach Meringue Pie, Green Tomato Pie, Gooseberry Pie, and Mince Pie was a recipe for Rhubarb Pie.

I wondered if Hazel Jackson would have approved of this recipe. Or if she had some magic of her own she would have added.

quotes from Presidential Cook Book adapted from the "White House Cook Book," The Saalfield Publishing Company, New York, 1907, preface, pp. 285, 288

Rhubarb Pie

Cut the large stalks off where the leaves commence, strip off the outside skin then cut the stalks in pieces half an inch long; line a pie-dish with paste rolled thicker than a dollar piece, put a layer of rhubarb nearly an inch thick deep; to a quart bowl of cut rhubarb put a large teacupful of sugar, strew it over with a saltspoon of salt and a little nutmeg grated; shake over a little flour; cover with a rich pie-crust, cut a slit in the centre, trim off the edge with a sharp knife, and bake in a quick oven until the pie loosens from the dish. Rhubarb pies made this way are altogether superior to those made of the fruit stewed.

Presidential Cook Book adapted from the" White House Cook Book," The Saalfield Publishing Company, New York, 1907, page 296

Gramma's Pie Crust

Makes one 10" shell

1-1/2 c. sifted flour
1/2 tsp. salt
1/2 c. Crisco
3 T. ice water

Mix flour and salt. Cut in Crisco with two knives until it looks like cornmeal. Add water a little at a time. Flour board well. Roll into 10" circle. Prick crust thoroughly. Bake until light brown in 450 degree oven.

Give Me Some Sugar

Marge's lovely sweet potato pie.

Majestic Marge in her 1950s garb.

Marge Taylor is one of those people whose spirit matches her lovely face.

We also met on the set of "The Majestic." The movie took place in the 1950s and Marge looked fabulous in those fashions. The A-line dresses along with matching hats, gloves, and purses suited her perfectly. Besides being beautiful, she was the type of person who never complained despite the painful high heel shoes, the drizzly, cold weather, or the long hours waiting in the extras tent.

We extras spent about six weeks together and became good friends. After the movie was done filming in Ferndale, many of us got together once a month for nearly a year and had potlucks and gossiped about the movie. At two of the potlucks, Marge brought her sweet... potato... pie. When you say sweet potato pie, you have to draw those words out as if you are dreaming of heaven. Because that's what Marge's pies are - heavenly.

At one potluck, I asked her for the recipe because if I had a choice between pumpkin or sweet potato pie, I'd take sweet potato.

Marge shyly smiled, her brown eyes squinting almost shut, and exclaimed, "I don't use a recipe."

Oh Lord. How was I to recreate this sweet treat? I can wing it when it comes to vegetable sautés where the exact amount of the ingredients doesn't matter, but it was my understanding that baking was like a science project - it must be exact or fail.

When I initially thought of the idea for this book, Marge was one of the first people I wrote in my notes to interview. She lived down the street from an elementary school I was going to speak at, so I called her. This was my chance to get her recipe.

"I'll be taking photos while I interview you," I noted, "so you'll probably want to make a pie." Wink, wink.

"Maybe then I can pay attention and write that recipe down," she said. "You know, I'm always experimenting so they turn out different every time."

"I'll just have to have a slice and be the judge of whether it comes out good or not," I teased her. She laughed and agreed.

After my school presentation, I drove down the street to Marge's house, a dark chocolate pudding color with golden yellow trim the color of crust.

She greeted me like an old friend and showed me into the house. There, majestically sitting upon her dining room table was her sweet...potato...pie. It was as if a light from above was shining down on it.

Marge had made the pie the night before wearing a nice dress and pearls, like a good 1950s housewife.

"No apron," she said proudly. "My mother never wore an apron, and neither did my grandmother. Didn't get a speck of flour on me either."

Yet this time, Marge had to pay attention to how much ingredients she used so she could write down a recipe for me.

"I don't use recipes because they dirty up so many dishes! All that measuring, getting the measuring cup greasy. I just spoon the Crisco out of the can, look in the bowl, then decide if I have enough and spoon some more if I have to.

"I shoulda waited until you got here to show you how I made the dough."

Instead, she reenacted the scene. With her mocha brown hands, she gently scooped up the imaginary dough and lightly pushed it into a ball. Marge suggested taking your rings off before making your dough ball. Bacteria and all. And don't overwork it.

"But how do you know it's overworked?"

"It feels stiff and you won't be able to roll it out."

"How do you know when to stop working it?"

"Stop when all the pieces in the bowl are together in a ball."

Aha! There was one mistake I had been making. I'd want all the itty bitty pieces that fell off my ball to stick back on, so I'd add more water, squeeze the pieces onto the ball and work it some more to compact it. It just made the dough tough and then I'd have to fight to roll it out.

Marge continued, "Then I set the ball aside and make my filling."

Ah, the sweet filling.

"I like to bake my sweet potatoes rather than boiling them," noted Marge. "The boiled ones have too much water in them and make the filling kinda runny."

Marge prefers red-skinned yams. She also steps up the amount of spices so that their flavors come through. And the other key is to combine white and brown sugar.

When Marge is ready to roll out the pie shell, she puts the ball on one of those cloths marked with circles the sizes of crusts, and puts some flour on top of the ball. Then she uses a rolling pin with a sleeve and rolls away and towards her stomach in a V motion. She then turns the dough a rotation and rolls in a V again until she has rolled it out to the size marked on the cloth.

Before I cut into Marge's sweet...potato...pie I noticed that the filling wasn't cracked like my pumpkin pies tend to be.

"I never have any trouble with cracking," said Marge. "I don't know why. Maybe it's the texture of the filling, or maybe some people use too much liquid."

"Does your crust get soggy?"

"No, I cook the pie at 400 for 15 minutes first, then I turn it down to 350 and slow cook it. People are amazed my edges don't burn."

"Do you use tin foil to cover them?" To prevent burnt edges I always put tin foil or these handy pie edgers around the outer rim, then removed them during the last 15 minutes. Pie rings work, too.

"No, you have to know your oven."

I guess I don't trust my oven like Marge does. Mine's a slow cooker, so I usually turn it up about 25 degrees and I still have to cook it longer.

Enough talk. I sliced a wedge and Marge topped it with whipped cream. With a cup of English Breakfast tea on the side, I took my first bite. Yes! The heaven that I remembered from the potluck! The texture was perfect. Marge's crust was super thin and a touch crunchy. But it held the filling well.

Marge looked at me a bit shyly, waiting for my response.

"This is so good, Marge."

She smiled then revealed a secret. "You know, I always have a bit of extra dough left over so I put it into a little Pyrex dish and pour some filling in to make me a sample. That way I can taste it before I bring it to a potluck."

Being the experimenter that she is, Marge came up with another people-pleasing version of her sweet potato pie by putting a pecan layer on top. She beats one egg, then adds 2 tablespoons of clear Karo syrup, 1/2 cup sugar, and whips it up good with 1 cup of pecans. She pours it over the uncooked sweet potato pie filling and then bakes it. She cuts back on the amount of sweet potato pie filling she puts in, so that the pecan layer won't spill over the edges.

"That means a bigger sampler for me!" She roars with laughter.

"Marge, I think for you it's all about the samplers." She laughs heartily again.

At Thanksgiving, she bakes her traditional sweet potato pie but substitutes heavy cream or half-and-half for the evaporated milk, and adds more butter. "Thanksgiving is no time to cut back. You can diet later." She also grates in orange zest, about a tablespoon, to give it a slight citrus flavor. Then she serves it topped with vanilla ice cream.

Each Thanksgiving she meets her family - three sisters, two brothers, two daughters, two sons, and a bunch of nieces and nephews- at her sister Regina's house in San Bernadino.

"They call me the head cook during Thanksgiving because I supervise the kitchen." Marge bakes about eight pies and a couple of cobblers.

"We're sitting all over my sister's double wide, at counters, tables, on sofas. We eat in shifts. It's so much fun. Some of my family wants to do it twice a year, but once is enough for me. Keeps it special."

Marge grew up in Orlando, Florida in the 1930s and 40s in a big family with five girls and three boys. She's the second child in the lineup. Her mother sold Avon products and was the disciplinarian in the family. Her father was a Pentecostal minister. As a small girl she pushed a box up to the stove to watch her mother cook.

One day, when her mother went to sell Avon, she decided to

surprise her by cooking biscuits.

"I had a tin with 30 spots to fill, so I thought I'd better use a lot of flour. I dumped the whole five pound bag in a bowl then added water. I made the dough into balls and filled each of those spots. They came out like rocks! I wanted to soften them so I poured a pitcher of water in the tin and recooked them. They didn't soften so I poured another pitcher on them. They dried out in the oven. I was so upset I cried when my mother came home. My mother asked, 'What's the matter?' I said, 'I wanted to surprise you and make biscuits.' She tried not to laugh when she saw them. Then she taught me how to make biscuits."

Marge shook her head. "That was the worst day in my cooking life."

From there on out Marge starting cooking and experimenting. She got so good her mother told Marge that her pies were better than hers. When she was about 20 years old, her mother turned the kitchen over to her, and Marge cooked for the family.

"One reason why I think I became a good cook was because we had to eat all our meals at home. Black people weren't allowed in white-owned restaurants. And the ones the black people owned we called greasy spoons. The food wasn't very good. They were trying to get by, so they put fillers in their hamburgers and such."

Marge chuckled at the bad experiences she had eating at greasy spoons. "It was fast food, but not because you could get it fast!"

After her grandmother's funeral service in 1976 in Orlando, Marge and her family went to Morrison Cafeteria, a place she wasn't allowed into as a kid. She ordered seven meals.

"My brother saw the waiters bringing all these trays to us and asked, 'Who's ordering all that food?' Me! I told him. I'm making up for lost time!"

With now three slices missing from the pie, I could see how beautiful her pie plate was. Made of ceramic, it was a deep golden color, nearly the same as the pie itself, with a brown rim painted on the inside just below the crust line. I commented on how perfectly it complemented her sweet potato pie.

"I always use this pie plate for my sweet potato pies," she said. Then she went off into another room and came back with a pie plate with pictures of apples on the inside bottom of it. "This one I use for my apple pies. I don't mix them."

Like Marge, I, too, have special pie plates. There's a small ceramic one that an old neighbor in McKinleyville made that I bought at her tag sale. It's blue with a dark blue rim, perfect for blueberry pies. I have an elegant butter-yellow ceramic plate for my peach pies. And an apple pie-shaped plate that has a tall lid with a protruding apple on the top which serves as a handle. It's great for deep dish apple pies. Only problem is, there's a fantastic recipe for apple pie printed right on the bottom of the pie dish. So when you put your crust in, it covers the recipe!

Marge insisted I take home a few slices. Otherwise she'd have to freeze a slice or two since it was just her and her husband eating the pie. "But pie freezes just fine," she assured me. "Just wrap it in tin foil then stick it in a freezer bag. Then when you want a piece of pie, just take it out of the wrappings and microwave it. It's not as good as fresh-baked, but it's still pie!"

My lucky husband was going to have a real treat for breakfast.

As I drove home, the image of mixing white and brown sugar emerged with great symbolism. I hark back to when Marge talked about growing up with prejudice. How she got yelled at by her mother for sipping the water out of the white people's drinking fountain. How a friend of hers who wrote a love note to a white girl got thrown into a river to drown while his father watched, threatened by the KKK not to tell. How there was a cross burning in the front yard of the elementary school she attended when she was in third grade. How when she and her husband moved to Humboldt County in 1959, the hotel clerk didn't want to rent a room to blacks.

I asked her if she hated white people after seeing so much bad treatment.

"No," said Marge, pointing to her second husband in the other room, a white man. "My father taught us to do unto others as you would want them to do unto you."

Maybe that's why Marge has no trouble mixing white and brown sugar.

Makes for a sweeter pie.

Single Pie Crust

1-1/4 c. flour
1/2 tsp. salt
1/2 c. shortening (prefers Crisco)
4 T. ice water

Blend first three ingredients until flour appears beaded. Add approximately 4 tablespoons ice water. Do not over mix. Form in a ball. Let rest for 15-20 minutes while you're making the filling. Flour your board and roll to a 9" crust. Lift and put into pie plate and crimp edges.

Marge's Sweet Potato Pie Filling

4 small baked sweet potatoes or yams
1 can 15 oz. evaporated milk
1 c. sugar, half white granulated sugar/half brown sugar
1/2 stick butter
1 T. nutmeg
1 T. cinnamon
1/4 tsp. ginger
2 eggs
1 T. vanilla
pinch of salt (about 1/4 tsp.)

Bake, peel, and mash potatoes. Add all other ingredients and beat with electric mixer until all are blended well. Pour sweet potato mix into crust. Bake 10 to 15 minutes at 400 degrees. Lower oven to 350 degrees and cook for 30 to 35 minutes.

Made with Love

Sylvia rolls the dough out with a redwood rolling pin.

My husband and I bought our first home in a McKinleyville development, attracted by the affordable price and large yard.

We vowed it was just a starter home and we'd be out in five years. We stayed eight. Finally, I couldn't take the fog anymore.

The absence of sun in McKinleyville was starting to depress me. Some days it'd be foggy until 3 p.m. then blue sky would finally break open, stay for a few hours, and at 5 o'clock, just as Dan was getting home, the fog would come rolling back in. Fog in the morning was fine for writing, but in the afternoon when I wanted to go outside, it was cold and clammy. It always felt like a wet grey blanket hung over my head, pushing my eyebrows down into a frown. It was getting to the point where I was telling Dan constantly, "If we don't move inland, we're moving out of Humboldt County completely."

We searched for houses in Blue Lake, yet they were run down, scarce, or out of our range. Finally after a few years of looking, we found a 1+ acre lot in the Glendale area and built a home. It was amazing how a few more hours of sunlight could brighten my mood and change my 'tude.

About four years after Dan and I had moved, I saw an old McKinleyville neighbor, Mariann Hassler, at a Career Day fair at College of the Redwoods representing the local Carpenter's Union.

"What are you working on now?" asked Mariann. "Wes still brings up the pumpkins you took pictures of for a book you were working on."

One Halloween, Mariann's husband, Wes, put out some pumpkins on their front porch. They never carved them, just let them sit there. Time marched on, and it was well into the summer, and those pumpkins were still on their porch. Not a spot of rot on them. I was fascinated by their staying power so I borrowed them for a book project.

"Never became a book," I confessed. "Turns out someone else

beat me to the idea. It did become a photo essay of the cycle of pumpkins for a kids magazine though."

"Oh good," said Mariann.

"Actually, I'm working on a pie book."

"Pie?" Mariann's face lit up at the mention of the word. "Sounds fun."

"Yeah, I'm meeting a lot of neat people."

High schoolers started pouring into the gymnasium so I told her to say hello to Wes and I scooted over to my display table.

Five hours later, the fair and wrap-up luncheon finally over, I was walking back to my car in the drizzle when Mariann pulled over and rolled down her window.

"Been thinking about your pie book," she said. "Do you know Sylvia Tidwell?"

"No I don't."

"She makes the best pies and is someone you should talk to. She was my surrogate mom when I moved here. She didn't have a lot of money, but felt if she could make something special by hand for her children, like cookies and pie, that they'd have love and everything would be okay."

That touched my heart. I had to meet this person.

Sylvia lives in Fieldbrook, a community which spreads from the backside of McKinleyville and creeps into the outskirts of the Glendale area. What attracts people to this area is sunlight.

To get to Sylvia's house, I drove on windy, dippy Fieldbrook Road through the redwoods, past the school, past the barn, past the winery until I came upon Wagle Lane. I turned onto Wagle Lane and took a left at the fork. I realized I never asked Sylvia for her house number and wondered how I'd find it on this gravel road. I came upon a compound of houses with outbuildings and a chicken coop. When I saw the goats and sheep, I figured I was in the right place. Mariann had told me about all the animals Sylvia owned. Her driveway was just after the big tree encircled with tires.

Sylvia waved me over to her house. A generator hummed loudly, so we ducked inside. She was quite agile for a woman of 70.

She brought me into her kitchen where she had already started a pie. The huckleberry filling was heaped in a bowl, berry juice leaking into the sugar creating a vibrant, almost fuchsia, stain. The yellow-y dough was partially blended, awaiting the final wet ingredients. Leaning against a window was a wooden sign that read, No Matter Where I Serve My Guests It Seems They Like My Kitchen Best. Fresh eggs from her chickens lay on the countertop.

Before she focused her attention on the pie, she showed me a basket of emu eggs. Teal green in color, they looked like avocados, only bigger.

"Last year my female laid 30 eggs," said Sylvia. "The male sits on them and hatches them you know." Apparently it takes 50 days for an egg to hatch, although Sylvia never had any eggs that did. Her female starts laying eggs around Thanksgiving. After she lays one, the male pecks at her so that he can take over and sit on the egg. From a kitchen window we spotted him in the corner sitting on one now.

The female sauntered into view like some prehistoric creature. "That one is real curious. She hangs around while I garden, then snatches my glasses and hat!

"You gotta watch their feet though. It's like they have dinosaur nails. She ripped my pants with them."

Sylvia's pie crust recipe called for one egg - a chicken egg.

The crust recipe Sylvia was about to show me, she confessed, was not the one she used as a young housewife.

"I didn't like to invite people over for pie because I didn't like the crust. It would just, arrr." She made a face and waved off the thought. "You have to have patience. Those other crusts I'd just want to throw out the door!"

When Sylvia discovered the Never Fail Pie Crust 20 years ago in a cook book, she started inviting people over for pie.

Since this was April and raspberries weren't in season yet, Sylvia was making a huckleberry pie with berries she had picked last year and froze.

Huckleberries are ripe from late August sometimes into October. There are two kinds she picks, blue huckleberry and black huckleberry. The blue are a little bigger, but Sylvia prefers the black because of their flavor. I had heard of red ones too. One of her neighbors has given her access to his property so she picks from his bushes.

"I don't go there alone though," said Sylvia. "There's mountain lion and bear." Although she hasn't seen one yet, she has seen evidence, aka poop.

"I sold whole pies at a booth in Fieldbrook for $8 each. Someone came up and said, 'Eight dollars?' I said, 'Have you ever picked and cleaned huckleberries?'"

We gathered around the bowl where the pastry waited to be finished. Sylvia mixed an egg in the water and slowly poured it into the bowl. "Oops. Almost forgot the vinegar." She added apple cider vinegar and stirred. "People look at me funny when I add vinegar, but you don't smell it or taste it once it's cooked."

When she was done mixing, the dough was a lovely yellow color and had a pliable consistency. She stuck it in the refrigerator.

Next she explained what she did to make the filling. The back of a tapioca package was her source of the filling recipe, substituting huckleberries for blueberries. Sylvia prefers tapioca to flour to firm up her filling.

"I've got a friend who don't like the taste of pure huckleberries, so sometimes I put a cup on top of an apple pie so you get the flavor of both. The berries turn the apples a pretty blue-red. I've thought about entering that one in the county fair."

She cleared the peninsula and laid out a large wooden cutting board. She plunked an unusual, oversized rolling pin on the tile countertop. Grains of wood striped the length of the pin in dark brown and honey.

"My grandpa made that for me out of redwood. He was a mill wright in Korbel."

"It's heavy!"

"It don't bother me," said Sylvia, "except after making 91 chicken pot pies like we did the other day."

The rolling pin left subtle tread marks in the dough, releasing a pleasing butter scent. As she rolled out the dough, Sylvia remembered picking berries as a kid. "But my grandma never made jam out of them. I saw a neighbor who made a fresh loaf of sourdough bread, spread thick with butter and jam, and I told myself that when I have kids, they will never be hungry for jam."

Sylvia has five grown children who have never gone hungry for jam or any sweet treat, for that matter.

"When they were young I couldn't afford to run to the store to buy cookies, so I made my own and had cookies and milk for them after school."

People in Fieldbrook know her as the "Cinnamon Roll Lady" because she made cinnamon rolls for school fundraisers, and also sold them at booths along with her huckleberry pies. Recently, she brought some rolls to the local volunteer fire department after they put out a fire across the road. She wanted them to know how impressed she was with their professionalism. "None of them cussed the whole time they were putting out that fire."

Before dumping the filling in, she showed me a trick to keep the bottom crust from getting soggy. She mixed two tablespoons of flour and one of sugar and layered it on the bottom.

The whole time she was assembling the pie, I was mesmerized by her hands. Some of her knuckles were knotty like burl on redwood trunks, but her fingers were long and graceful. It wasn't so much how her hands looked, it was how they gently pressed the crust into the plate, how they held the knife and cut the excess dough off, how they tucked the upper crust under the lower one as if tucking a blanket under a baby.

I recalled Mariann telling me, "I used to watch her butter toast and think she should be doing it faster. But then when you really watch how she spreads the butter slowly, she just does it with so much care. Makes you think what's the rush anyway."

Sylvia paused to show me how she fluted her edges. First she floured her fingers, then she pressed a deep divot in the dough. "You want to make it come a little below the rim of the pie plate so it keeps the juices from spilling out."

She poked a fork all over the top, sprinkled sugar on top, then slid the pie into the oven.

Since Sylvia never makes just one pie, she rolled out another single crust for a banana cream pie for her son who lives next door. There was plenty of leftover dough which she rolled out, buttered, sprinkled with sugar and cinnamon, rolled up and sliced to make miniature cinnamon rolls. "My kids love these."

While the pie and miniature cinnamon rolls baked and cooled, Sylvia said a prayer before we ate our tuna sandwiches made with home-canned albacore tuna.

Over our sandwiches, we talked about osteoporosis, her kids, Fieldbrook, Mariann her "adopted daughter", her 70th birthday party at the Grange. We discussed the war on Iraq, and crazy people in the world. She was so easy to talk to, I could see why Mariann claimed her for her surrogate mother.

"I bet you have lots of adopted children," I teased her.

"You've gotta share what you've got."

She sliced the still warm huckleberry pie and sent me home with half.

"You'll have to come back when my raspberries are ripe."

I thanked her for her generosity, and said good-bye to her pie-eyed dog, Blue.

Never Fail Pie Crust

Makes 4 shells (5 if you stretch it.)

4 c. flour
2 tsp. salt
1 T. sugar
1-3/4 c. shortening (Sylvia prefers Butter flavor Crisco for its color)
1 T. apple cider vinegar
1 egg
1/2 c. cold water

Mix flour, salt and sugar. Cut in shortening. Mix vinegar, egg, and water then slowly pour into the flour mixture. Work it into a ball with a fork and your hand until there's no flour at bottom of bowl. Separate into 4 balls and roll out.

Huckleberry Pie Filling

4 c. huckleberries
1 c. sugar
1/4 c. tapioca
1 T. lemon juice

Mix sugar and tapioca together. Add berries and lemon juice. Pour into pie dough.

The Pie Guy

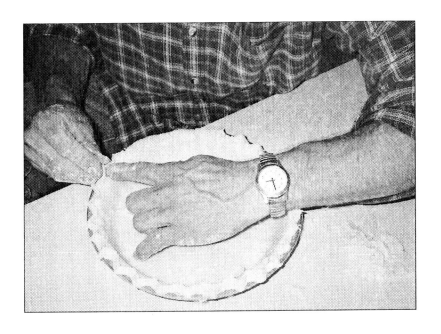

John Bush demonstrates crimping.

When I was a kid living in Connecticut, my friend's mom used to tease me about how I pronounced pecan. I said "pee-can" instead of "pe-kahn."

"A pee can is what you put by your bed to urinate in," she said. "A pe-kahn is a nut."

I've said pe-kahn ever since.

I pride myself in baking a good pecan pie because it's Dan's favorite at Thanksgiving. I've even made chocolate pecan pie, and brandy pecan pie. Both drew rave reviews from my most discriminating customer. But, I was still having trouble with my crust. For some reason, when I crimped the edges, the zig-zaggy pattern would seem to melt into something nondescript by the time the pie was done cooking. I couldn't fathom how people made crimped edges stay crimped.

Would I be able to get help from a guy?

"As far as I'm concerned, Fanny Farmer is the only cookbook you need," said John Bush as he walked over to a split log bench carrying the cookbook as if he was carrying a 2x4 on his shoulder. He took a break from cabinet making to talk to me about pies.

"Here," he said, pointing to the Pies & Pastries section. "Read this and you'll know how to make good pies."

I noticed the book opened naturally to the Best-of-All Pecan Pie recipe, the page smeared with a greasy thumbprint.

"I use this one," he said, "but hers is too runny so I add another egg."

John is not the kind of person you'd meet and think was a pie baker. He's charmingly shy, lean, and builds houses by day. But what did I expect from a man who bakes? A heavyset gregarious sort who wielded a rolling pin better than a hammer?

I had met John at a Halloween party Dan and I and a bunch of our friends put on at a barn in McKinleyville. It was the perfect setting for a Halloween party with bales of hay strewn about, red-and-white checked table cloths on picnic tables, a staging area with scarecrows and pumpkins, and tacky colored lights strung every where. If one spark had touched a piece of hay, the whole place would have gone up in flames, but the thought of it just added to the edginess of Halloween. We had a band and a costume contest. Gypsies, clowns, and sailors danced in a mosh pit of the macabre and howled to the song "Werewolves of London." It was a blast. John was dressed like a pirate and I was a cave girl.

When my friend, Barrie Love, told me John dropped by a pecan pie for their Thanksgiving dinner, my mental notebook went "check-plus."

"From scratch," she added. Wow, I thought. My admiration for John jumped a notch.

When I asked John about pie-making, he said, "Barrie thinks it's the funniest thing that I make pies."

"Why?" I asked, "Do you wear an apron?"

"No!" he retorted, "'cause I'm a guy making a pie."

Growing up in a family of seven children, six boys and one girl, John said there was no gender when it came to cooking in his house. "My mom gave each of us kitchen duty one night a week." With seven kids, his mom made out on that deal.

When John got married at age 23, his grandfather gave the newlyweds The Fanny Farmer Cookbook. John's bible.

"This can't be the one your grandpa gave you," I said, eying the new paperback.

"This is a replacement. My first one had pages stuck together and tape on the cover," which he noted the ex-wife now has.

John baked his first pie - pecan - during their first year of marriage. He's been making pecan pies ever since. "Now I make them for Thanksgiving, Christmas, and randomly throughout the year."

John's got a few secrets. After 22 years of pie baking, he rarely measures the ingredients anymore. Before even making the crust he puts a glass of water with ice cubes in the freezer. Then he makes a traditional crust with Crisco ("Don't use the butter-flavored stuff. It has a funny fake taste. I like the white grease.") He reenacts how he makes the dough, sticking his fingers in imaginary ice-cold water and flicking it with his fingers.

"You don't want the dough too wet. You want it crumbly, like gravel. Then when you roll it out, it's already flaking when you pick it up."

"You know, Sonja said you make the BEST pecan pies." John looked at the ground in his "aw shucks" way and smiled at the thought of his daughter, Sonja, bragging on him.

I, however, didn't want to rely on hearsay. I'd have to have some physical proof. But getting it turned out to be a test in patience.

Between his life stuff and my life stuff, it was like trying to fit a round crust in a square pan. I'd be free, but he'd be out of town. He'd be in town, but I'd be gone. I'd be polite and not push him, thinking, "He knows I want to bake a pie, he'll call when he's available." Then he'd be polite and not call a married woman. This went on for about two months to the point of ridiculousness. The build up was getting so overblown (for me at least, since I felt like a Type A Sadie Hawkins pursuing the shyest boy in the class), that the possibility for a let down hung in the air.

I was about to choose pie abstinence when at last, a mutual Saturday was clear for both of us. Dan was going with his buddy, Alan Gunn, to climb Mt. Shasta, so I thought I'd have a pecan pie waiting for his arrival home on Sunday.

"Your place or mine?" asked John. Only problem was his place above the Love's garage didn't have an oven, and you can't cook a pie on a George Foreman grill. We borrowed the Love's kitchen so he wouldn't have to pack all the ingredients over to my place.

At about 1:30 p.m., I went manned with a clear-glass pie pan and my trusty dough blender. After a run to the grocery store for missing ingredients, we were ready. A small audience of Patsy Jackson, Barrie and her husband, Wade, and son, Wendell, were there to witness this culinary event.

While a bowl of water and ice, and the can of Crisco, were being chilled in the freezer, I measured the flour and salt into a bowl. We added the Crisco and I cut it in to the flour with my dough blender.

"You don't need that," he said. But I didn't want to use the two-knife method so I continued on. "Okay stop," he said after I barely blended it.

"Are you sure?" I asked. "I thought it needed to look like

little peas."

"Na," he said. "It'll get mixed in when we add the water."

He flicked the water in by shear guesswork and tossed it around a bit until the dough began to stick. This was the part that always made me anxious.

"Don't worry about it," he assured me.

Being the measuring sort, I had to see how eyeballing the dough worked. His looked too clumpy to stick, but somehow it rolled out okay, even though it needed patching and stuck to the counter because we didn't put enough flour down first. John slid a knife under his circle and worked it off as if removing old wallpaper. I did the same and surprisingly, it didn't crack when I lifted it. Phew. Phase I complete.

He slid the crust into his clear glass pie plate, tamped it down, then poked it with a fork all around the sides and bottom. John was after a flaky pie crust, and was under orders from Wade that it be crunchy, because, "John's pie wasn't leaving his kitchen."

Then came the part I'd been waiting for - the crimping. John meticulously went around the outside and crimped the edges with defined, pointy scallops. It was beautiful.

While I was watching John's hands, a high-school moment surfaced. Remember sitting around with your girlfriends talking about what kind of guy you thought was cute? Some of my friends liked business men in suits. Others thought men in uniform were the cat's meow. I liked the guys who could wear Levi's and confidence like a second skin. Just a photo of a man in worn-out jeans - especially if he was bare-chested and holding a baby - would send my heart a pitter-pattering. Never in a million years did I think a guy making a pie could be so danged cute.

I snapped out of my high school daze when John picked up a fork and proceeded to press it into his masterpiece! Smush, smush, smush. No more beautiful crimps.

He admired his creation as an artist who, alas, had captured the afternoon light on canvas.

"See how the pattern matches the pecans."

He did have an artistic point there - edge decorating was up to each individual dough artist. My friend Sharon, who's a fabulous cook, confessed she simply cannot crimp, so she cuts out dough leaves and lines the edge with them. We all have our little tricks to distract people from our weaknesses.

John precooked his crust for 10 minutes before putting the filling in. I didn't. I don't like overdone crusts. Like with brownies and cookies, I'd rather err to the undercooked than the over cooked side. Barrie agreed, "I like the soggy bottom crust of chicken pot pies." So I opted to do just a few fork-pricks on the bottom.

The filling part was easy, although we almost forgot the vanilla. John likes to add extra nuts to his filling. "Even though the recipe says pecan halves or coarsely chopped pecans, I use both. It's kinda like concrete where you want all the spaces filled in."

We slid the pies, one over the other, into Barrie's 1951 O'Keefe & Merritt oven, a cheerful nostalgic thing that's white with red knobs.

We checked the pies after 30 minutes, but the filling was still wavy when I rocked the pie back and forth. We decided to leave them in longer since there were two pies instead of one which probably was affecting the cooking speed. In the meantime, we popped open a few bottles of cheap Chardonnay for a group taste test to see if the $9 wine was better than the $2.50 wine.

That's when the 1950s domestic scene of perfection ended.

While wrapped up in comparing wines, we almost forgot the pies!

John's came out of the oven with the crust blackened all around and underneath. (Mine looked pretty good. My crimp pattern, sans fork presses, was still in tack.)

While the pies cooled, more wine poured.

The Love's invited us to stay for dinner so we could all taste test John's pie. I envisioned a Campbell's soup moment when we'd all place our bites in our mouths at the same time and rub our bellies and say, "um um good," in unison.

Instead, the phone rang - John's son, Nathan's, car had died at the side of the road so off he went to rescue him. We ate without him, drank another bottle of wine while the cat hissed from a chair and swatted at the dogs circling around the table. Should we wait for John or just slice into his pie without him?

In walked John and Nathan, sweaty and bleeding from walking through the Himalayan bushes to get home. John shoveled down some barbecued salmon. Now can we have pie? Nope, had to take the son home first. All we could do was wait for his return. More wine?

About 10 giddy hours after starting this whole pie-making process, we cut into John's pecan pie.

Wade was happy. The crust was crunchy all right - what didn't stick to the pie plate shattered under our forks! We analyzed why that happened and thought maybe the filling leaked out and caramelized. Nevertheless, the rich filling was fantastic, and a little homemade whipped cream cured our crust woes.

So my search for the perfect crust - and the secret of crimping - continues. And although John reassured me that measuring didn't matter, I wondered if it did just a bit.

When I stood up from the table, I knew I shouldn't drive home. Too much wine. I got as far as the Love's couch. Everyone else turned in except John who sat with me for hours until I sobered up enough to drive. It was 1 a.m. - almost twelve hours after starting the pie - when I took my pie home, plunked it down on the countertop and climbed into bed. Never even turned on a light.

A phone call at ten in the morning woke me up.

"How ya doing, honey?" It was Dan's cell-phone voice.

"I'm hungover," I moaned.

"Did you have fun making your pie?"

"Too much."

"We're coming home," he said. "Skunked again."

Dan's third attempt at climbing Mt. Shasta was thwarted by high winds. So much for the pie being a celebratory reward for his reaching the summit.

I hung up and crawled back into bed. If Dan were here he'd cheerfully say, "I feel sorry for the nondrinkers, because right now's the best they'll feel all day."

Dan got home late that afternoon. Curled up in my overstuffed chair, I listened to the tales of Dan the Mountain Man. Apparently it was so windy (50 mph plus) he couldn't walk without gripping the icy slope. Hikers' tents were shredded. One hiker warned him that "it was another world up there."

Sensing his frustration, I gave him my '50s mom response, "Better have some pie, dear." The cure all. He disappeared into the kitchen and in no time I could hear the rattling of the pie plate on the stove top.

"What's with this crust?" he called to me. "It's breaking up when I cut it. I don't like that it's falling away from the filling either." I've created a taste test monster.

"Want some?" he asked when he came back into the living room.

"No thanks." My appetite still hadn't returned.

Dan gave thumbs up on the filling, although he felt the crust was too thin and dry.

"But a pecan pie in May is still a treat," he said while sampling his second piece.

All I could do was hope he wasn't so famished by his climbing attempt that he'd eat the whole thing, so I could try some in the morning. When my appetite returned.

John's Rich Pecan Pie

One 9" pastry dough

1 1/2 c. flour
1/4 tsp. salt
1/2 c. shortening
3-4 T. cold water

Mix the flour and salt. Cut in the shortening with a pastry blender or two knives. Combine lightly only until the mixture is crumbly. Sprinkle water over the flour mixture, a tablespoon at a time. Mix lightly with a fork, using only enough water so that the pastry will hold together when pressed gently into a ball.

Filling:
4 eggs
1 c. dark corn syrup
1/2 c. dark brown sugar

4 T. butter, melted
1 tsp. vanilla
1-1/4 c. mixture of pecan
   halves and pieces

Preheat oven to 425 degrees. Line a pie pan with the rolled-out dough. Prick bottom with fork (if you want it crunchy) and set aside. Beat the eggs in a bowl with a fork or wire whisk. Add the dark corn syrup, dark brown sugar, melted butter, and vanilla, and blend well. Stir in the pecans, then pour the mixture into the pie shell. Bake for 15 minutes, then reduce the heat to 350 degrees and continue baking another 15-20 minutes, or until outer edge is set and the center slightly quivers. Don't over bake. Let the pie cool a bit. Serve with whipped cream.

Tasha's Tipsy Pecan Pie

One 9" pastry dough

2/3 c. brown sugar
1/3 c. butter, melted
3/4 c. corn syrup
1/3 c. brandy
1/2 tsp. salt
3 eggs
1 c. pecan pieces

Prepare pastry. Preheat oven to 375 degrees. Beat sugar, butter, corn syrup, brandy, salt and eggs with hand beater. Stir in pecans. Pour into pastry-lined pie plate. Bake until set, 40 to 50 minutes. Refrigerate until chilled. Refrigerate any leftover pie.

Chocolate Pecan Pie

For Chocolate Pecan Pie, use the above recipe only leave out the brandy, increase corn syrup to one cup, then melt two 1-ounce squares of unsweetened chocolate with the butter.

Too Tart

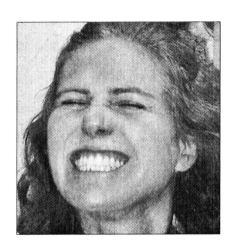

Boy howdy, that's tart!

Okay, so I like a pie that's a bit tart. That is, until I made an apricot pie.

My writer friend, Mary Nethery, told me her mother makes wonderful apricot pies. I had never thought of an apricot's use beyond being a dried fruit snack. So the idea intrigued me, and one day on the way back from a hike to Guthrie Creek trail with Dan, we stopped at the fruit stand at Fernbridge. They were selling bags of gorgeous, sunset-yellow apricots. Peach season was still about a month or more away so I decided to make an apricot pie. According to Betty Crocker, the fruit is a good substitute for peaches.

I don't know if it's my way of reducing the calories and therefore reducing the guilt, or if there always seemed to be a wasteful amount of sugar at the bottom of the bowl when I make filling, but for some reason I started cutting back on the sugar amount suggested in recipes. My justification was that I wanted to let the flavor of the fruit come through, not the sugar. So, when the recipe called for 1-1/4 cup of sugar for the filling, I cut it back to 1 cup.

What a difference a 1/4 cup could have made!

Although the consistency and color of the apricot pie was pretty, the taste was super tart. In the fruit's defense, it may not have been completely ripe. Still, I couldn't believe that I actually admitted I didn't like a piece of pie! I scrunched my nose when I ate it, and passed on seconds.

Dan, on the other hand, loved it!

There's an unspoken rule in our house that when it comes to dessert, we divide it evenly. So when I told him I didn't like the apricot pie, it was like giving a king free reign to invade my country. He seized my territory, slice by slice. One day he had a piece of pie for breakfast, lunch and dinner. We had Wade and Barrie Love over for a barbecue on Memorial Day and I served the last three thin slices to them with vanilla ice cream. I just ate the ice cream. Wade wished that the crust was crunchier, and Barrie said it was good as long as she had a hunk of ice cream with it. Dan didn't say a word because he was too busy licking his plate!

I might give the apricot another chance, but there's one thing I will do differently. I'll try the fruit to see if it's sweet, and if not, I won't cut back on the sugar!

A few weeks later I spoke with Helen Scuri, Mary's mom, and told her about my awful experience. Helen suggested next time I use drained canned apricots halves that have already been sweetened in light syrup.

"A little amaretto or rum helps, too," she said.

Apricot Pie

Two 9" pie crusts

1 c. sugar
1/4 c. all-purpose flour
1/4 tsp. ground cinnamon
5 c. sliced fresh apricots
1 tsp. lemon juice (unless the apricots are tart to start)
2 T. butter

Prepare pastry. Heat oven to 425 degrees. Mix sugar, flour and cinnamon. Stir in apricots and lemon juice. Turn into pastry-lined pie plate. Dot with butter. Cover with top crust and cut slits in it. Seal and flute. Bake until crust is brown and juice begins to bubble through slits, 35 to 45 minutes. Serve with vanilla ice cream.

Amaretto Apricot Pie

Two 9" pie crusts

1 large can of apricot halves in light syrup
1 c. sugar
3 T. minute tapioca
2 T. flour
dash of nutmeg
1/4-1/3 cup amaretto
1 egg yolk

Drain and reserve syrup from apricots. In a bowl, mix sugar, tapioca, flour and nutmeg. Add apricots. Add back 1 cup of syrup. Add amaretto. Put in pastry-lined pie plate and top with crust. Cut slits in top then brush with egg wash and sprinkle with raw sugar. Bake in preheated oven at 400 degrees for 15 minutes then turn it down to 350 degrees until browned to your liking, about 40 minutes.

Suggestion: You may want to get two 15 oz. cans of apricots if purchasing them from a store versus using home canned apricots. I used two 15 oz. cans of apricot pieces and it turned out nicely. It's better to have more fruit than not enough. Also, I tried draining the juices and didn't get one cup, so I just dumped both cans of apricots in with the juices.

Making Multiples

Making pies for The Westhaven Blackberry Festival.

On the first Saturday of the month, Old Town Eureka stages an art walk called Arts Alive!. I went one March and saw artist Adrienne Werth displaying her beautiful watercolors. We used to work together at an ad agency, so we're always interested in what the other is doing in our "lives after advertising." She asked me what I was working on.

"I'm putting together a pie book," I said.

Her pink lips, the color of the magnolias in her painting, spread with a wide grin and her hazel eyes twinkled. "Pies? That sounds neat. I always wanted to know how to make multiple pie crusts."

My mind flashed to my recipe box and the muddied photocopy from the Spry container that has a table of ingredients measurements for one to four pie shells. I had attempted to make four shells one time and it turned out to be a disaster - the dough turned out too dry.

"Yeah," said Adrienne. "When I want to make two two-crust pies, I have to make the dough for one pie, then start again and make another batch."

"I'll ask the Westhaven ladies," I said. "Stay tuned."

The Westhaven Ladies Club is a group of women who make blackberry pies every year to raise money for the Volunteer Fire Department. They bake about 800-900 pies from October to May, although not all of them are blackberry. They buy marionberries and mixed berries from commercial suppliers, while the wild blackberries they get from local pickers. Pies - baked and unbaked, whole and by the slice - plus jellies are sold at the much anticipated Blackberry Festival which is held the last Sunday of July.

In the fifteen years I lived in Humboldt County, I never got to the festival for one reason or another. With my mission to find out how to make multiple crusts, I had to go. And who could pass up real blackberry pie?

I called Florence Couch who is the treasurer of the Westhaven Ladies Club to see if I could talk to her about the Blackberry Festival. I admitted to her that I've never been to the festival - nor eaten a real blackberry pie. "I've only made Himalayan pies."

"Don't say that word around us," cautioned Florence.

Himalayans are like the bad relative who came to visit and never left. Both the California native blackberry and Himalayan blackberry are from the rose family, although it's the Himalayan thorns that are tougher and hurt more when you stretch for that juicy berry dangling just out of reach and get impaled on a vine.

Himalayans were most likely imported into Humboldt County for their fruit and have become an invasive, thorny lesion on the landscape ever since. Mounds of bushes smother pasture fences and choke native plants. We had them in our yard and after an initial aggressive chopping, I've been hacking at relentless sprouts ever since. My neighbor resorted to a goat to help clear hers. But I must admit, I do like the flavor of the fruit. And since the berries are so big, picking enough for a pie takes no time at all. But maybe I like Himalayans because I've never tasted the native blackberry.

"We're making our last batch of pies tomorrow," said Florence. "Come on down to the Fire Hall. You can see how our assembly line works."

Westhaven is one of those little towns that I just zip by on the way to Trinidad, the fisherman's town where I go to get smoked salmon, eat oyster omelets at the pier, or hike Trinidad Head rock. I drove north on 101 past Clam Beach and took the 6th Ave. exit to the Westhaven Fire Hall. It was 9:30 a.m. and the apron-clad volunteers were already set up in their assembly line for the final baking, hoping to make about 75 pies in an hour-and-a-half.

At one station, berries were being scooped into the flour and sugar mixture for the filling. At the next station, crusts were being rolled out. At another, two ladies were filling the pie plates and putting on the top crust, then off the pie went to the edge crimping station. The tops were then marked so they can tell what filling is inside. One hole in the center of the crust is wild blackberry. Two holes is marionberry. One hole with an "M" made with fork pricks is mixed berry. Once marked, another woman puts the pies into plastic freezer bags, and onto trays.

Florence's job was to stack the trays in the walk-in freezer. With her snowy hair, and woolly hat and gloves I dubbed her "The Polar Bear." That morning, the 10 busy workers turned out 80 pies.

The Blackberry Festival got started 43 years ago as a way to support the fire department which was established in 1950. A meeting was held to discuss fund raising ideas to support the new fire department. Everyone agreed they wanted their fundraiser to be different. Ideas were tossed around and aside until Mr. Moore, a blind man, started stomping his cane. "Make blackberry pies! There's plenty of berries around here." And so the festival was born.

The first year the firemen's wives and kids picked berries and volunteers made 200 pies. Now, with the addition of other berries, the Westhaven Ladies Club, with help from ladies from the McKinleyville Senior Center, make about 900. The profits not only support the Westhaven Fire Department, but the library, Rotary Club and the McKinleyville Senior Center also get a slice of the pie.

Florence has been helping with the pie making for 26 years. She has experienced trials and tribulations. One time they tried making the crusts with Butter Flavor Crisco and she said the color was not even. Another time they tried tapioca instead of flour for the filling, but it settled in the freezer. (Sometimes pies stay in the freezer for almost a year since the blackberries come in to season in June, right before the festival, so the berries picked this year are used in pies sold next year.) One year they lost the pies to a freezer mishap. The compressor had been turned off and wasn't discovered until a week later when a volunteer was setting up the Fire Hall for Tuesday night Bingo and saw juice running into the men's room.

Expenses have gone up too. Pie tins that used to be 12 cents are now 20 cents. A bag of blackberries that used to be $4 is now

$8 - $9, although this year may be as high as $10. And the cost of vanilla ice cream has gone up as well. Despite the increases, Florence was determined to keep the price of pies reasonable - $11 for a frozen or baked 9" deep dish pie and $3.50 for pie a la mode.

"We don't beg for donations," said Florence. "We may get discounts, but all of our ingredients are bought."

"So why don't you use (I had to say the "H" word) Himalayans?" I asked. Their sheer abundance would keep costs down.

"Seeds are too big and people don't like big seeds in their pies," said Florence, admitting that the berries do make good jelly.

"What's the difference in taste?"

"Blackberries are more tart." And less juicy.

Call it local lore, but people who pick blackberries keep the whereabouts of their patches secret. In all my picking years, I only saw a blackberry plant once on my friend, Tauni's, property in Fieldbrook. So I asked Florence where to find blackberries. All she could reveal was West End Road and Samoa Peninsula. I would just have to settle for a taste of previously-frozen blackberry pie. If it should be sumptuous, I'd have to get my fix from the Westhaven Ladies Club once a year until I could find my own patch.

I purchased a pie, and was ready to head out, contemplating whether or not I should bake it tonight (because I couldn't wait to taste it) or save it for Memorial Day weekend (but then I'd have to share it), when the ladies invited me to stay for freshly-baked pie.

The crust was a beauty - golden brown and a touch shiny. Florence told me they brush mayonnaise on the top before sliding the pies in the oven. The color of the filling was so deep purple it was almost black. As for the taste - magnifico! I tend to like a little bit of tartness to my pies, and this was just right. Especially with vanilla ice cream. The only thing missing was a little runny juice (because it was used to make jelly.)

As a testament to how good these pies are, Florence recalled one woman who went to church on the day of the festival and by the time she made it over to the Fire Hall, the blackberry pies were sold out. So as not to miss out the next year, she showed up at 8 a.m. in her pajamas and rollers in her hair and bought her blackberry pies before church.

How does an extraordinary pie result from an assembly line? It all starts with the crust. Since I was on a mission to find out how to make multiple crusts, I just had to know how they made so many pies at a time. And watching the rollers and handlers in the assembly line, I saw that this crust was very pliable and never cracked from dryness. I spotted a metal mixing bowl on the counter big enough to bathe two babies in at a time.

"How many pies do you get out of a batch?" I asked Florence.

"Fifty two-crust pies."

She showed me the dough recipe concocted by Hans Giovanoli who owned the Cherry Blossom Bakery in Eureka for 30 years.

Hans got involved in the pie making when his wife saw an ad in the newspaper looking for volunteer pie makers. Hans, who was retired, called the number and got Florence. He told her he wanted to help make pies. There was silence on the other end.

"Do you think because I'm a man I don't know how to make pies?" he asked in his Swiss accent.

"You took the words right out of my mouth," said Florence.

Hans started helping about three years ago and claims there is no secret to making a good crust. Just don't manhandle it too much.

Hans's tip for browning the bottom crust is to add powdered milk to the dough. Florence tipped a cooked pie over and showed me how evenly the crust had browned. Hans only takes credit for the pie dough, not the filling (that's someone else's recipe).

A few days after taking my frozen blackberry pie home, the thought that it lay in my freezer was more than I could bear. Rather than waiting for a special occasion to bake it, I took it out, thawed it for an hour and popped it in the oven. But first, I brushed half the top with mayonnaise to compare the difference. The mayonnaise side was brown and shiny, and the other side seemed bland. I had learned a new trick for making a more eye-appealing crust.

As I savored a bite of real blackberry pie, I now knew why the locals preferred wild blackberries to Himalayans.

Thank you Westhaven Ladies!

For all you non-profits looking to bake pies for fundraisers, here's a 50 pie crust recipe. You'll need a scale!

50 Pie Dough

Makes 50 two-crust 9" pies

20 lbs. flour
14 lbs. Crisco
8 oz. salt
8 oz. white sugar
5 oz. powdered milk mixed with 1 gal. cold water

Rub the flour and Crisco together with your hands. Mix salt, sugar and powdered milk. Mix in cold water. Add to flour mixture and toss side to side. Refrigerate for about 2 hours.

This one's for you, Adrienne.

6 Pie Dough

Makes 6 two-crust 8" pies

2-1/2 lbs. flour
1 lb. 6 oz. Crisco
1/2 qt. water
1 oz. salt
1-1/2 oz sugar
2-1/2 oz. powdered milk

Rub the flour and Crisco together with your hands. Mix salt, sugar and powdered milk. Mix in cold water. Add to flour mixture and toss side to side. Refrigerate for about 2 hours.

(Still too many crusts? You can freeze the dough and thaw it when you need it.)

Going Topless

Hans prefers European pies.

Like sunbathers on the beaches of Cannes, Europeans are not ashamed to go topless. Even when it comes to pies.

"I prefer European pies to American pies," said Hans Giovanoli, former owner of The Cherry Blossom Bakery in Eureka. "They don't have any top crust."

Open-faced pies, or "flan" as they are called in Europe, substitute custard for the top crust.

Hans acquired his taste for flan when he lived in Europe. He was born in Soglio, Switzerland, the town where the movie "Heidi" was filmed. When he was four, his family moved to Chur.

"In Switzerland they stress learning a profession rather than going to college. So at 18, I went to a baking school in Lucerne."

He learned how to make yeast goods, cookies and cakes, and French pastries and desserts. In the summers he was a baker. In the winters, a ski instructor. He gave a private ski lesson to Fred Hillman, a relative of Nelson Rockefeller, and fate took a turn.

"Every time he fell, I yodelled," said Hans. "He got a kick out of it and said, 'America needs people like you.'"

Fred sponsored Hans to come to the United States. Hans came over on the Queen Elizabeth when he was 22 and worked at Lake Placid, New York. He started the Swiss ski school there and taught the Swiss way of skiing. (He hopped out of his chair to demonstrate.) In the summers he went to New York City and worked as a baker at the Hilton Hotel.

After five years in New York, Hans headed to Chicago to be a pastry chef and a weekend ski instructor. In Chicago he met his wife, Bertha, who was a lab technician. As much as they loved Chicago, they didn't want to raise a family in a city. Hans had dreams of starting his own business. While gleaning through trade magazines, he saw an ad for a bakery shop "in the heart of the American redwoods in Northern California."

"Do you know there's a redwood tree in the rose gardens in Soglio?" He showed me a photo to prove it. "The climates are similar."

In 1965 he bought the Cherry Blossom Bakery, moved to Eureka, and started living his dream. He and Bertha had two children, a son and a daughter.

"It's beautiful here, don't you think?"

When Hans ran the bakery, it had an outstanding reputation for desserts made from scratch. I had eaten slices of his Black Forest Cake served at birthday parties, and the flavor made you want to yodel.

Hans was in the bakery business for 30 years when he saw the writing on the wall - Winco, Costco - and retired.

"When those stores came in, and people could get a pie or cake for $7, I knew it was time," said Hans. "People want convenience, not desserts made from scratch."

Retirement hasn't slowed Hans down. The fit 75 year-older mows his neighbors' lawns and skis at Mt. Bachelor in Bend, Oregon where "People over 70 ski free." And yes, he still bakes regularly. At Christmastime he and Bertha fire up the commercial oven set up in their garage and bake dozens of cookies as gifts for friends using European recipes. He also helps make the dough for the Westhaven Blackberry Festival pies.

One reason why Hans prefers European pies is that, in his opinion, most people don't make a good pie filling. Hans poo-poos pie fillings made with flour. "It leaves a funny aftertaste and makes the filling rubbery. Berry pies must run a little."

"Flour is the old way of doing it. Cornstarch is better than flour. Tapioca doesn't leave an aftertaste. I use an instant stabilizer made out of dried sea weed and cornstarch." Hans gets the stabilizer through a baking supplier since it's not found at a grocery store. He gave me a plastic tubful, claiming it was enough to last a lifetime.

Still, Hans is open to new baking tricks. One thing he learned from the Westhaven Ladies is to brush mayonnaise on his pie crust and then sprinkle it with sugar to make it crispy.

Perhaps the Westhaven Ladies will learn something from Hans and go topless at the next Blackberry Festival. I meant the pies!

Hans's Open-faced Pie

1 pie crust
ground nuts (grind in meat grinder or food processor)
fresh fruit

Note: For the fresh fruit, Hans suggested apple (peel them first), rhubarb, apricot, blueberry, peach or prune. Do not use strawberries. Trust me on this one.

Custard topping:
3 eggs
1 c. heavy whipping cream, or half-and-half
4 T. sugar

Make a pie crust, put it in a plate, cover the bottom with chopped nuts, and then put in the fresh fruit. Bake it at 350 degree until the crust is brown around the edges. When it is still warm, pour the custard over the fruit and bake at 350 until the custard sets up and turns light brown. When done, sprinkle sugar on top to give it a shiny glaze. Total cooking time from start, about 1 hour.

Going Bottomless

Bottoms up!

"I don't know why I didn't think of this as pie," said Patsy Jackson, "but I've got this wonderful recipe for Soda Cracker Pie."

While Patsy was traveling in Europe in days past, she met a travel agent from America who gave her a recipe.

"When I heard the ingredients, I couldn't believe that it would turn out."

There was no flour. No Crisco. And no fussing with crust.

Well, it got me thinking, if there was no crust, was it a pie?

Turning to the dictionary, I found two definitions. The first stated that a pastry-lined dish was involved. Aka a crust. The second said "a layer cake with a filling of cream, jelly, or the like." That loose definition just blew the possibilities wide open.

"My daughter, Kendell, serves it in her restaurant in Seattle, only she calls it some fancy French name. People wouldn't order it if it was called Soda Cracker Pie."

Maybe because the image of soda crackers is not too appealing. Kinda like asking someone if they'd like a slice of sawdust.

Exactly what is a soda cracker? Again, I turned to the dictionary. Soda cracker: "a thin, crisp cracker prepared from a yeast dough that has been neutralized by baking soda." Oh, yummy! Essentially, a soda cracker is a good ol' Saltine. The cracker you ate as a kid when you had a tummy ache. Not something one would immediately associate with dessert.

Since I am in search of the perfect crust, I almost didn't include this recipe. But then some Zen person may read this book and surmise the perfect crust is no crust. Much like if you put a lot of energy into attaining a goal, the absence of that goal is what will bring the most happiness.

With Hans, we've gone topless. Now with Patsy, we can go bottomless!

Soda Cracker Pie

6 egg whites
2 c. sugar
1 c. soda crackers, crumbled
1 c. walnuts
2 tsp. baking powder
1 pt. of whipping cream
1 pt. of berries such as strawberry or raspberry

Mix sugar, crackers, walnuts and baking powder. Beat egg whites until stiff like a meringue. Add the dry mixture to the meringue and fold in. Pour into 10" spring form pan. Bake at 350 degrees for 25 minutes until light brown. When cool, place berries on top (if strawberries, slice them up). Whip up whipping cream with some sugar to taste. Spread onto berries. Frozen raspberries work too.

Rolling Pins Are Flying

Every third Saturday in July, people gather in four towns in four countries to throw rolling pins.

It's called the Stroud International Brick and Rolling Pin Contest which is held between Stroud in Gloucestershire, England, Ontario, Canada, New South Wales, Australia, and Oklahoma.

The first contest started as a brickthrowing contest between Shroud, England and Shroud, United States. Both towns had Brickworks in common, and so as to "cement" their relationship, they started this contest in 1960. When it was found out that two other Shrouds existed, the contest opened up to Canada and Australia in 1961.

Australia suggested that a rolling pin throwing contest be added for the ladies, and in 1962, women were hurling 2 pound rolling pins, discus-style.

All the rolling pins used in the contests are made in Australia and shipped to the other Shrouds.

So how far can a woman throw a rolling pin?

The record is 156'4" held by England and the United States respectively. Although, I bet if a woman's pie crust didn't roll out properly right before her throw, you could add another 10 feet.

Strawberry Fields Forever

A roadside stand in Fortuna offers fresh strawberries.

Dan's been gone for almost a week now. He and a friend, Kip, went up to Alaska to backpack. They were being flown by a bush pilot into the wilderness and left for days to fend for themselves. I was worried about grizzlies eating him, but he assured me as long as he could run faster than Kip, he wouldn't be eaten.

We'd been out of phone contact until last night when he got back to the hotel in Anchorage.

"I'll never have to do that again, thank you very much," he said, laughing at the wild experience.

Apparently, hiking in the bush was way more difficult than he imagined- no trails to speak of so they had to force their way through miles of thickets. In the hotel shower, he was picking five days worth of splinters out of his skin.

Then in the next breath he said, "This was the most incredible trip. I want to bring you up here."

"I don't want to hike in the bush," I said meekly.

"No, no, no, not that. There's lots of other things to see up here."

"Can we take a train ride?" I asked. I had always romanticized about taking a train through the countryside. Besides, a train would enclose and protect us from the mosquitoes that are rumored to be so big you needed a baseball bat to swat them off.

"I got brochures for you to look at," he said. A silence, then, "I miss talking to you."

I couldn't wait for him to come home. And what better way to greet him than with a pie! I had two days to come up with an enticing combination of crust and filling that would insure we'd do more than just talk.

To the kitchen lab!

A flat of strawberries beckoned to be processed. Strawberries. The love fruit. Webster's definition alone conjures up thoughts of love-making: "the fruit of any stemless, rosaceous herb of the genus Fragaria, consisting of an enlarged fleshy receptacle" (then skip the part about bearing small, dry, hard thingies on its exterior).

I had gone down to Fortuna to view gardens on the heather tour. Deer don't care much for heathers, so I planned to plant more of them, and wanted to get ideas. While in Fortuna, I stopped by Saechao strawberry farm off Eel River Road. It's a business that started in Hydesville about three years ago by a family from Thailand, and since it did so well, the family expanded their venture in Fortuna. The strawberries are piled high in the baskets, and are big and red, inside and out.

I bought a flat thinking I could make an open-faced custard pie using Hans's recipe.

In my excitement to try something new, I felt adventurous and thought I'd try a new pie crust recipe as well, one for a precooked pie shell. That was my first mistake. For some reason I thought the pie shell was only going to be cooked once. Well, the custard pie gets baked, with the fruit in it, but the problem is, when the custard is poured in after that, it goes back into the oven. Cooking the shell twice made for one very overdone crust. I can sort of deal with a crunchy crust, but the filling had to make up for it. My strawberry custard filling was awful.

First of all, strawberries were the wrong choice. The juices seeped into the custard making a sickly pinkish brown color, reducing the love fruit to a turn off. Secondly, the custard tasted eggy when my tastebuds expected sweet. I rechecked Hans's recipe, and had followed it exactly, but I simply didn't like the taste. Perhaps using half-and-half would have been better. More sugar would have helped too. And one less egg. (Don't worry. The recipe in has been adjusted.)

Now I was stuck with a gross strawberry-custard pie, which I couldn't serve my honey. So on Sunday, the day before his arrival, I decided to make another pie. Since I had a lot of strawberries left, I turned to Hans's 6 Crust Pie Dough recipe.

Hans's recipe was in pounds and ounces, so first I converted the amounts to cups, teaspoons and tablespoons using the trusty conversion chart on my refrigerator; 2-1/2 pounds of flour to 5 cups, 1 pound 6 ounces Crisco to 2 3/4 cups, 1 ounce salt to 2 tablespoon, etc. Then I got out a whopper-sized bowl and followed his recipe.

It noted to mix the flour with the Crisco with your hands. At first it was fun feeling the silky flour and greasy shortening on my skin. Then it keep sticking to my hands and coating them like those wax hands you see at carnivals. All I wanted to do was get it off of me! After washing the gunk off my hands, I then added the watered milk mixture and blended it with a spatula. The glop in the bowl looked like mush, not like dough at all. I touched it and it stuck to my finger like a booger. I tasted it and it was salty. Now what?

I rechecked the recipe amounts and then started adding flour by the 1/4 cup until I added another 1-1/2 cups of flour! It started to look and act like dough, but something was terribly wrong. I covered the bowl and shoved it in the refrigerator and called Hans. No answer. Arg!

One thing about being a writer is you never know what situations will inspire a story idea, a poem, or in this case, a limerick.

> There once was a gal from Nantucket,
> Who attempted a crust but then f--- it!
> It came out too soupy,
> And made her so loopy,
> That she threw the whole mess in a bucket!

The baskets of strawberries still mocked me on the countertop. Like a wild-eyed mad scientist, I washed a mixing bowl and tried again. This time I turned to Betty Crocker and used her pie dough recipe. No refrigeration needed. Just mix it and roll. Instead of making my tried-and-true Strawberry Glacé Pie, I got sidetracked and made a strawberry-rhubarb pie for Barrie to taste test to see if it tasted like Gramma Hazel's. Dan wouldn't be home until tomorrow.

I intended to just drop the pie off at the Love's house and go home and make Dan's pie. Well, I should've known better. Whenever I go to Barrie's, I don't want to leave. It's so fun there with people coming and going, animals swirling about my feet, all set against brightly colored walls (Dan calls it "Barrie's Big Top") that it's hard to pull myself away. So I stayed for dinner, and was able to witness the reaction to the pie first hand.

Wade served up the slices, putting his and Wendell's in a bowl so they could drown theirs in milk. Wade said his grandma used to serve him straight rhubarb pie in a bowl with milk. He'd always ask for seconds. Wendell gobbled his down. Barrie loved hers, too. It wasn't tart, like she remembered her Gramma's to be. But that seemed to be okay with her.

"If a pie's too tart I'd have to cut it was some sort of cream," she said. "Not this one. It's de-LICIOUS. And look at the pretty crust. It's perfect!"

I had to admit, this was the prettiest pie I'd ever made. Using the advice from the Blackberry Festival ladies, I brushed the top with mayonnaise and sprinkled it with sugar. It looked like a magazine photo. The crimping was gorgeous, the filling, a pretty deep rose color. I marvelled at the beauty before me after such a failure of a day with Hans's pie dough.

Wade liked his slice, but highly suggested - several times - that I make a straight rhubarb pie next time.

"That's my favorite flavor," he said, grinning like a ten year old.

I left a slice for John Bush and Patsy, and took the last slice home to Dan. His welcome home pie was reduced to a slice. There was no time to make another.

On Monday morning, he came home from Alaska, all sleepy from his late night flights and dreamy from what he claimed was the best trip he had ever taken. He was covered with scrapes and bruises from hiking through the bush, but it was a small sacrifice for the sites he saw.

"Alaska grips you," he said. "It's just incredible. The scale, icebergs, daylight until 11 at night. Everybody is so nice and helpful. It's like you're back in the '50s." He barely unzipped his suitcase when he said, "Honey, when I retire, we're going back for three months."

I offered up the slice of strawberry-rhubarb pie which he devoured like a hungry grizzly bear. My little love dart took effect.

Later that day, Patsy called to thank me for her slice of pie.

"I have to tell you, that was the most delicious pie I ever had. I felt wicked eating it."

Then she said the words I had been waiting for. "It was better than Gramma Hazel's."

My strawberry-rhubarb pie had risen from the doughy glop, like a phoenix rising from the ashes.

Sing pie birds, sing!

I got ahold of Hans a few days later and asked, "What did I do wrong?"

Essentially, ALL OF THE CONVERSIONS.

"A cup of flour is 4 ounces," he said. "A cup of sugar is 8 ounces. It's different for each ingredient."

"OH NO!" I cried. "That's why it turned out so bad!"

We laughed at my misunderstanding.

"You have to use a scale. Do you have a scale?"

"No, I just have a measuring cup with ounces and a conversion chart, but I guess it's for liquids."

"I'll get you my conversion chart from my teaching days," said Hans, "so you can measure the American way."

I told him about my awful strawberry custard pie, too.

"You don't want to use strawberries with custard. Pudding with strawberries. That's what you use."

I really blew it.

"But the custard still tasted eggy to me."

"I use less eggs than Bertha when I make my custard, so just use one less. And maybe one more soup spoon of sugar."

"Soup spoon?"

Hans laughed. "Oh, you have different sizes of spoons here, too. Ours from Europe is big."

All I could think was a half of bag of flour and a half a can of Crisco is a small price to pay for what could have been a disaster if readers used my conversions. I'd have more than egg in my face. I'd have raw, sticky dough thrown at me, too.

The next day I still had three baskets of strawberries left and some were starting to fuzz.

With the remaining good strawberries, I made a strawberry pie without the rhubarb, and this time, made a lattice top since the filling color is so pretty. Dan gave the crust a 10, but the filling without the rhubarb tang, wasn't as exciting, so he only gave it a 7. I should have stuck to my tried-and-true Strawberry Glacé Pie.

Welcome home, honey.

Strawberry-Rhubarb Pie

Two 9" pie crusts

1-1/3 c. sugar
1/3 c. all-purpose flour
Pinch of dried orange peel (or fresh grated peel)
2-1/2 c. sliced strawberries
2 c. rhubarb cut into 1/2 inch pieces
2 T. butter

Prepare two crust pastry. Mix sugar, flour and orange peel. Mix rhubarb and strawberries in bowl. Preheat oven to 425 degrees. Put half the fruit mixture in the pastry-lined pie plate. Sprinkle with half the sugar mixture. Put in the rest of the fruit and sprinkle with the rest of the sugar mixture. Top with butter dabs. Brush top with mayonnaise and sprinkle with sugar. Cover edge with foil and put in oven. Cook 30 minutes. Remove foil and cook another 15 minutes until crust is brown and juice begins to bubble through slits.

Strawberry Glacé Pie

One 9" baked pie shell

6 c. strawberries, stems removed
1 c. white sugar
3 T. cornstarch
1/2 c. water
1 5.5 oz. pkg. cream cheese, softened
2 drops vanilla

Bake pie shell. Mash enough strawberries for 1 cup. Mix sugar and cornstarch in 2-quart saucepan. Slowly stir in water and mashed strawberries. Cook over medium heat, stirring constantly, until mixture thickens and boils. Boil and stir one minute, then cool.

Beat cream cheese with vanilla until smooth. Spread on bottom of cooled pie shell. Fill shell with remaining strawberries. You can either position them in whole with tops down, or slice them. Pour cooked strawberries mixture over top. Refrigerate until set, about 3 hours.

Razzle Raspberry

My main pie taster, Dan, tests a forkful of raspberry pie.

When raspberry season rolled around in June, I got a call from Sylvia, as promised. Raspberries are one of my favorite berries. My Grandpa Lazutin grew rows of raspberry bushes in his garden in Massachusetts. As kids, my brother, sister and I ate the berries right off the bush. I knew they were a special treat because of the way my mom used to say "raspberries" much as people who covet caviar say "caviar" in that long, drawn out dreamy way.

Many grown-up years later I learned from Mom that Grandpa planted his garden on a piece of property he didn't own, which just so happened to belong to my other grandpa.

I'm sure he was just enhancing the property value.

With my mouth watering with anticipation of eating raspberries, I went to Sylvia's house on one of those rare Humboldt County summer days when you wake up to sunshine and the temperature gets in the high 80s. Mariann was supposed to join us for lunch, but was ill. So Sylvia and I cut to the chase and sat down for tuna sandwiches. Sylvia had inadvertently switched plates, and I got her sandwich. This led to a surprising discovery - tuna fish and horseradish are a zippy combination!

"I don't like real hot stuff, but I like horseradish," said Sylvia. "I put it on my tuna one day and decided it was good."

We talked about her recent trip to Europe; how beautiful the Alps were; how her family tried to coax her into the Mediterranean Sea which she did with much reluctance; how she was impressed with Spain's beauty. She visited lots of countries in three weeks.

"We didn't stay in one hotel for more than two days," she said.

One thing she missed about home was butter.

"They dip their bread in olive oil. I couldn't wait to come home and spread butter on my bread."

I, on the other hand, couldn't wait to try her raspberry pie which sat on the countertop waiting for us to finish our sandwiches. It

89

was a gorgeous bright red.

Sylvia spread Cool Whip on the top then cut us each a slice along with a slice of cherry pie. She had gone to Willow Creek and picked Bing cherries, and had so many that she decided to bake a pie. I was not one to say no to two slices of pie.

I sunk my fork into the raspberry one first. Bliss! The raspberry tartness melded perfectly with the whipped cream. This was one divine pie.

After finishing the raspberry pie, I turned my fork to the cherry pie. I didn't want to tell Sylvia I didn't care for cherry since I was trying to keep an open mind. The only cherry pies I've ever tried were made with canned filling which glowed an unnatural red. When I think of cherry flavor, I think of cough syrup, so that could be another reason for my dislike.

Well, my dislike was confirmed. The cherry pie slice paled in comparison to the raspberry. I didn't like the consistency of the filling, or the deep, sick red color. Now I knew why George Washington cut down the cherry tree! To keep Martha from baking cherry pies!

Sylvia looked down at her piece with concern.

"I should have used more sugar," she said. "And I'm not sure Bing cherries are right for pies. They're eating cherries." She took another bite. "We probably should have started with cherry first, then ate the raspberry."

I agreed. Like in a wine tasting, you start with dry and work your way up to sweet. The sweetness of the raspberry killed the subtleness of the cherry. But I'm still not convinced that I should try cherry again.

After lunch we went outside into the satiating sunshine and visited her emus. Emu-emu, the male, was very friendly. He came right up to us at the fence and stared at me with golden brown eyes. His long, curved neck and small head reminded me of a snake, and I was on-guard in case he should strike out, but he never did. I checked out his three-toed feet which were black and very prehistoric, looking as if they could tear dinosaur flesh in one swipe. Emu-emu, the female, was taller than the male, and strutted back and forth making a drumming sound in her throat. She was rather aloof, and Sylvia was perplexed by her behavior.

"What's the matter with you, Emu-emu? You hot?"

Sylvia hosed the two down. We fed them dandelions then retired under shade for lazy afternoon conversation.

I tore myself away at about 3 o'clock, leaving with two slices of raspberry pie in my hand. Dan was needing the SUV for another trip to Mt. Shasta. He and Alan were making their fourth attempt at summitting. He gobbled down his slice before leaving, grunting and moaning with pleasure at its flavor. Then in a swoosh, he was packed and gone.

The next day, I stayed near the phone, wondering when his call from the top of Mt. Shasta would come, or if he'd report another aborted mission. I had to pick our dog up from the groomers, and upon returning, there was Dan's message.

"Hello, gorgeous! I am calling from the top of the 14,162 foot summit of Mt. Shasta, c'mon! Oh, baby, this is what it's all about right here."

Actually, I preferred to climb the mountain of Cool Whip on Sylvia's raspberry pie, c'mon!

Red Raspberry Pie

(adapted from a recipe by Mary McCullough, "Fieldbrook Favorites" ,1977); a 2004 Humboldt County Fair Best of Show winner!

1 single crust, baked
1 c. water
1 c. sugar
4 T. flour
5 T. raspberry Jell-O, (strawberry Jell-O will do)
2 baskets of raspberries, crushed or whole
Whipped cream or Cool Whip

Bake pie shell. Bring water, sugar and flour to a boil. Stir in Jell-O. Pour over berries in baked pie shell. Top with whipped cream. Refrigerate.

Sugar Coma

Wave a magic wand.

When my Dad turned 65 he was diagnosed with diabetes. The excesses of retirement living in sunny Arizona, and genetics, had finally caught up to him.

Then a few months ago, my Mom was diagnosed. I wished I had a magic wand to make their diabetes go away. But luckily, they can control it through diet and exercise.

When I went in for my yearly female physical, I mentioned to my doctor that both my parent now have diabetes, my grandpa had it, and that I am sensitive to sugar. I also noticed that my eye site in my right eye was blurring in what seemed like a short time. Blurry vision was my dad's first sign. So out of caution, my doctor suggested I get my blood sugars tested.

I kept putting it off since I didn't want to find out any bad news before going to Dan's high school reunion in June. I didn't want to find out before camping during the 4th of July weekend either. What if I couldn't have any s'mores? Yet after that camping trip was over, I went for my test.

All I could think of is what if I have diabetes and I can't eat pie?

After fasting 12 hours, the nurse-guy drew my blood. I'm a weakling when it comes to needles and seeing my own blood, so I covered my eyes, felt the sting, and sniffled after it was over. I tried to coax a coloring book and crayons out of the nurse, but he wouldn't give in to my tears. Instead he made me drink this orange glucose liquid then held me captive at the hospital for two hours until I could get my second reading - another draw of blood. I offered my other arm, turned my head, and winced when the needle went in. Got a free bagel out of him this time though.

I was in no hurry to get my results, yet the not knowing gave my mind time to think of all the drawbacks of having diabetes. I'd have to prick my finger and test my blood every day. I'd faint! I'd have to cut out just about my entire food intake. Half the stuff in my refrigerator and pantry would have to be tossed. Adios Aunt

Jemima syrup! I couldn't have my glass of wine before dinner. Bye-bye cocktail hour! And the irony of writing a book about pies and not being able to eat them would be torture.

So after about a week, I called my doctor.

Results: 111 fasting. 119 recovery.

Normal.

That night Dan and I had Barrie, Wade, Patsy and John over for dinner. For dessert I had a slice of mixed berry pie with a scoop of vanilla ice cream. And for that moment, it was the best pie I'd ever eaten.

Mixed Berry Pie

Two 9" crusts

1 c. sugar
1/3 c. flour
1/2 tsp. cinnamon
4 c. berry mixture (blueberry, blackberry, raspberry make a nice combination)
2 T. butter
mayonnaise

Prepare pastry. Heat oven to 425 degrees. Mix sugar, flour and cinnamon. Stir in berries. Turn into pastry-lined pie plate and dot with butter. Cut slits into top crust and brush with mayonnaise. Cover edge with aluminum foil to prevent over browning. Bake 30 minutes then remove foil and bake for another 15 minutes until crust is brown and juice begins to bubble through.

The History of Pie

Pie has been around since the ancient Egyptians. The first pies were made by early Romans who may have learned about them through the Greeks. These pies were sometimes made in "reeds" which were used to hold the filling, but were not eaten with the filling.

The Romans must have spread the word about pies around Europe as the Oxford English Dictionary notes that the word pie was a popular word in the 14th century. The first pie recipe was published by the Romans and was for a rye-crusted goat cheese and honey pie.

Early pies were predominately meat pies. Pyes (pies) originally appeared in England as early as the twelfth century. The crust of the pie was referred to as "coffyn". There was actually more crust than filling. Often these pies were made using fowl with their legs left to hang over the side of the dish to use as handles. Fruit pies or tarts (pasties) where probably first made in the 1500s. English tradition credits making the first cherry pie to Queen Elizabeth I.

Pie came to America with the first English settlers. The early colonists cooked their pies in long narrow pans calling them "coffins" like the crust was called in England. As in the Roman times, the early American pie crusts often were not eaten, but simply designed to hold the filling during baking. It was during the American Revolution that the term crust was used instead of coffyn.

Over the years, pie has evolved to "the most traditional American dessert." Pie has become so much a part of American culture, that we now commonly use the term "as American as apple pie."

Excerpt from The American Pie Council website: www.piecouncil.org.

□

Red, White and Blueberries

Warm blueberry pie made with Wolfsen Farms blueberries.

When the 4th of July rolls around, I think of blueberries.

Maybe it's because of the ads that appear in women's magazines for 4th of July picnic desserts that are made of Jell-O and Cool Whip. Layered parfaits with strawberries, whipped cream and blueberries. Red Jell-O cubes topped with Cool Whip and blueberries. Or cakes decorated like the American flag.

I couldn't celebrate the 4th without a blueberry pie, so like a teenage boy drawn to fireworks, I revved up my 1964-1/2 Mustang and headed to my favorite U-pick farm - Wolfsen's Organic Blueberry Farm in McKinleyville.

Owner Herb Wolfsen is a balding, round man who, with his blue coveralls, looks like a big blueberry.

Herb greeted me with a smile and a bucket.

"Whatcha looking for?" he asked.

"I'm wanting to make a blueberry pie," I told him.

Two women walked up to get their buckets of berries weighed.

"Can she taste one of your berries?" Herb asked them.

"Sure!" The women held out their buckets.

I peered in. "They're so big!" I exclaimed gazing at the nearly marble-sized berries. Tasty too.

"That's what I want," I told Herb.

Herb pointed me to the last six rows of bushes where the Collins grow. I found the opening in the bird netting and proceeded to pick. The berries plunked into my bucket like coins falling from a slot machine. I had hit the jackpot!

A few families were out picking that day. I overheard one mom telling her boys that blueberries reminded her of summer. A child proclaimed that he found the bush with the "mostest" berries to which his mom told him to try to get more berries in the bucket than his mouth. Another girl said she ate a green berry "on accident."

I went up and down the rows, finding branches of ripe blueberries that the families had overlooked.

With my bucket nearly full, I weighed in. Three and one-half pounds, plenty for a pie and beyond.

I meandered home in my Mustang, soaking in summer, looking forward to baking a fresh blueberry pie. I got out my blue ceramic pie plate, the one I only use for blueberry pies, and whipped up a pie like magic. This time I added two tablespoons of butter to my regular Crisco recipe and piled the blueberries extra high.

Dan couldn't wait to let the filling cool, so it ran a bit, but mixed splendidly with the vanilla ice cream. Upon tasting, he proclaimed the crust to be my best ever.

Fresh berry pie with my favorite guy on 4th of July. This is what summer is all about.

Note: Herb Wolfsen doesn't claim to be a baker, but he thought the Collins are a little too sweet for pies. "The flavor blows out and doesn't hold up to baking as well as others." He suggested his Bluerays or N51Gs which have a stronger flavor.

If you're not getting your blueberries from a supermarket, and have a choice, go for tart over sweet, strong over mild. That way the blueberry flavor won't get lost in the sugar.

Butter & Crisco Crust

Makes two 9" crusts
2-1/4 c. sifted flour
1 tsp. salt
3/4 c. Crisco plus 2 T. butter
1/3 c. cold water

Mix flour and salt in a bowl. Cut in Crisco. Cut in butter until size of peas. Sprinkle in water, 1 tablespoon at a time. Toss lightly with a fork. Form dough into a ball and divide in half. Make two balls. Place dough on floured surface. Roll from center out to form 9" circles.

4th of July Blueberry Pie

1/2 c. sugar
1/3 c. all-purpose flour
1/2 tsp. ground cinnamon
4 c. fresh blueberries
2 T. lemon juice (if berries are tart, then cut to 1 T.)
2 T. butter

Heat oven to 425 degrees. Make pastry. Mix sugar, flour and cinnamon. Stir in blueberries and lemon juice. Dot with butter. Moisten edge of bottom crust with water. Cut slits in top crust and cover filling. Seal and flute. Cover edge to prevent over browning (aluminum foil strips work), but remove during last 15 minutes of baking. Brush with mayonnaise. Bake until crust is brown and juice begins to bubble through slits, about 40-45 minutes.

Doo-rang, Doo-rang, Meringue

Helen spoons her lemon filling into a baked pie shell.

Most people steer clear of meringues. All it takes is one deflated meringue and their ego deflates as well.

I was not quite sure why I never made meringue pies. Perhaps they reminded me of too many late nights at diners after college parties where three-day old pies spun around and around in lighted cases while my eyes spun around in my head. Or perhaps the topping seemed unnatural, like spray foam.

Mary Nethery convinced me that I should talk to her mom about lemon meringue pies.

She held her hands about seven inches apart and said, "Her meringues are this high, I swear."

Children's fiction writers have a tendency to exaggerate the truth (don't I know), so I had a little bit of the "oh, sure" voice going on in my head. But knowing Mary, she was probably within an inch of the truth. A six inch tall meringue pie was still amazing.

Putting my laisez-faire attitude toward meringues aside, I drove south of Eureka to Elk River Road then took a right onto Zanone Road. Helen greeted me shyly at the door. She's a petite woman who's one-quarter Irish, one-quarter French and half Polish, and can lay claim to being second generation American and a Humboldt County native. Helen was born in the old St. Joseph's Hospital on F Street in Eureka and grew up on Elk River Road across from Zanone Road, in her grandfather's house.

Her grandfather owned a grocery store in Elk River called Whelihan's. When he had a stroke, the family took over and ran the store until the Depression. During the Depression they extended credit to customers, and when the customers couldn't pay, they couldn't afford to keep the store open. The building is no longer there.

Helen told me the street used to be called Forbes Street (in the 1900s the area was known as Forbesville), but the fire department decided to rename it Zanone Road since there was already a Forbes

Street in Cutten. Her husband got so mad at the change that he tore the sign out. But the fire department won out.

Helen still lives in the house where she and her late husband, Gino first moved. Helen knew Gino since they were children. When they married, they moved right next door to Gino's parents where his Italian-born father grew lettuce for local restaurants. They raised their three daughters here.

I wondered what it was like growing up in Elk River.

"When I was a kid we cleaned our clothes in a copper boiler on the wood stove by stirring them with a stick," said Helen. "We had an old cooler, no fridge. We creamed milk to make butter and buttermilk and had pigs we slaughtered and made lard from, and that's what we used in our pie crusts."

Helen's mother was a good baker and used to cook on an old wood stove. Helen learned to cook by watching her, then she'd fool around with the recipes. Even today, many of the foods she makes are from scratch, partly because she has terrible allergies. She's allergic to corn so she uses safflower oil instead of corn oil in her crusts, and tapioca flour, arrowroot or potato starch instead of cornstarch in her fillings. She couldn't eat the lemon meringue pie she was preparing because it had cornstarch in it. But that doesn't stop her from making them for others to enjoy.

"This is an anytime pie," said Helen who gets together with her family once a month to stay in touch and often makes this pie for their gatherings.

I was anxious to give it a try. A golden single crust sat on the counter, ready to be filled. Mary arrived and joined in on the goings-on.

"I've got some brownies for you, Mary," said Helen.

"Where?" asked Mary, perking up. "She makes the BEST brownies."

Mary cut some squares for us to eat.

"You frost your brownies?" I asked Helen.

"That's the ONLY way," insisted Mary. She cut some more squares and wrapped them so that she could take them home to freeze.

"Little stinkers ate my brownies when I was gone," said Mary referring to her son and his girlfriend. "And they were MY birthday gift."

While we munched on frosted brownies with chocolate chips and nuts, Helen got the filling started at the stove. She added the initial ingredients to a sauce pan, and with a wooden spoon, stirred constantly over medium heat. The egg yolks already gave the filling a puckerish yellow color. When Helen asked me how much lemon I wanted, I said, "Put it all in."

Helen transferred the spoon to me when the filling started to thicken so I could see how it should feel.

"Stir faster," she said. I could hear a slight scorching sound as the filling tried to stick to the bottom. We turned the heat down to keep brown chunks from forming.

When it was thick, we took the pan off the heat and added butter, lemon juice and grated rinds and let it sit. Now for the meringue.

A heavy duty Kitchen Aid was recruited to do the task of whipping the meringue. Helen started off with egg whites and cream of tartar and whipped them on medium speed. Then she put one tablespoon of sugar in at a time and gave it time to blend in.

"Oooo," said Mary, watching closely. "Is that what you do? Maybe that's why mine doesn't come out as tall as yours, Mom."

"Are you dumping your sugar in all at once?" asked Helen.

"Yep."

"One tablespoon at a time."

I could see the whites starting to froth up.

As girls do, we got a teensy bit sidetracked with talking. That short time was enough for the meringue to transform into a bumpy froth. Helen's face fell like flat meringue.

"This is not how it's supposed to look," she said as she spread the meringue onto the filling, her brow frowning. "It should be smooth, easier to spread."

She dabbed it on with a spatula and worked it with a spoon, making sure it touched the crust all the way around or else it would shrink during baking. I felt bad that it wasn't as fabulously fluffy as she wanted it to be - as she no doubt has made it perfect hundreds of times before.

Into the oven it went for 15 minutes or so, and when it came out, it was browned over and very textured rather than smooth, yet its sheer size exuded a presence bordering on regal.

We sat around her kitchen table and talked politics until the pie cooled and I had to get along to a potluck. My main taste tester, Dan, was in Phoenix caring for his father, but at the potluck, I'd have plenty of new tasters.

When I brought the pie in, meringue bulging high above the pie plate, all eyes widened.

"What you got there?" asked a guest.

"Lemon meringue pie. From scratch."

A collective "ooo" resounded around the kitchen.

"You make it?"

"No, a friend's mom, but let me know what you think of it. I'm taking comments."

Slices were passed around the kitchen and out to people in the backyard.

"I LOVE lemon meringue pie," said Sam. Her big brown eyes rolled with delight as she slid the sampling off her fork.

"Oh, God, this is good," said another.

A teenage girl didn't say anything, but helped herself to a second piece. Helen's pie was a hit.

Oil Pie Crust

2 c. sifted flour
1 tsp. salt
1/2 c. salad oil
3 T. cold water

Mix flour and salt together. Add all salad oil and mix well with fork. Sprinkle 3 tablespoons cold water over all. Mix in with a fork (if too dry add 1-2 tablespoons more of oil). Roll out between waxed paper.

Lemon Meringue Pie

Make one 9" single pie crust and bake
In sauce pan blend:

1-1/2 c. sugar	3 T. flour
1/3 tsp. salt	3-4 T. cornstarch

Mix in:

2-1/4 c. water	4 egg yolks

Mix until you don't see the yolks. Cook directly over medium heat, stirring constantly until mixture boils. (As thickens, turn down heat to prevent scorching.) When thick, take off heat.

Add:

2 T. butter	juice and rind from 1-1/2 lemon

Stir in until butter melts. Let sit.

For meringue:

4 egg whites	8 T. sugar
1/4 tsp. cream of tartar	

In mixer, beat egg whites until slightly frothy. Add cream of tartar. Beat until slightly thick. Add 1 tablespoon of sugar at a time until stiff and frothy. Put lemon filling in pie shell. Spread meringue over top of lemon filling. Make sure it touches the edges. Cook 15-20 minutes at 350 degrees. Cool away from draft (a chill may make the meringue fall) and serve when plate is cool.

Got the Blues Again

Picking at Lost Coast Blueberries is on the honor system.

Last year while driving back from A.W. Way campground near Honeydew, a little white clapboard tilted on the side of the road indicated there was a U-pick blueberry farm close by. We didn't stop, but I was curious how the Honeydew blueberries compared to the McKinleyville ones.

There was no better way to find out than to try some.

Since the Honeydew U-pick was about a two hour or so drive from my house, I thought I'd better give a jingle first to see if they were open.

"Praise the Lord!"

I thought I had the wrong number.

"Is this Lost Coast Blueberries?"

"Yes," said the man.

"When will your blueberries be ripe?"

"Oh, three weeks or so, mid June, they're a little late this year."

We had a cold, rainy spring, weather we should have gotten in January. But now that summer was here, we were getting some pretty hot and sunny days. But not as hot as Dan was experiencing. He was in Phoenix caring for his 86 year old father who had fractured his hip on Father's Day. His sister, Melinda, was in for a much needed break, so Dan was spending some time caring for L.P. He arrived on the hottest day of the year - July 10th. A recorded 116 degrees. I talked to him a few days later and it had gotten down to a cool 108. It served as a reminder why we both high-tailed it out of there like jackrabbits soon after we were married.

So while Dan was in Phoenix, I decided to take a Sunday drive down to Honeydew to pick blueberries. A quick phone call confirmed Lost Coast Blueberries was now open.

"Good morning. Praise the Lord." I had gotten the same man with the George Carlin voice.

"What are your hours?" I asked.

"We're open daily during day light. You can pick as long as you can see," he said. He told me to bring a container, and that everything was on the honor system - "just put the money in the jar. Two dollars per basket." I was advised to wear sunblock and a hat, and bring water since it could be 100 degrees out.

I headed south to Ferndale, stopped there for a sandwich at Village Bakery, drove through the Victorian Village which seemed even more idyllic when the sun was out, and took a left at the sign for Petrolia.

Here is where one of the most beautiful drives in Humboldt County begins.

If you can overlook the poor narrow, windy roads, and ignore the jostling and tousling that the lumps and bumps inflict on your car, you will witness some of the most stunning views. Sprawling ranches. Towering straw-colored hillsides that meld into a blue sky filled with puffy white clouds. Dramatic descents down to the ocean where California's happiest cows enjoy grazing on the stunning ocean-front property. (Imagine what life would be like for a cow who gets to watch sunsets while chewing to the sound of ocean waves.)

Along the roadside daisies danced in the breeze. Queen Anne's lace was just starting to pop open. Fuchsia fox gloves dangled from their stalks. And pink sweet peas billowed everywhere. This countryside is so sensual that all I could think about was pulling over and making mad-cow love to a rancher dude.

I traveled on, past the grocery store in Petrolia, past the Hideaway bar, over the bridge and beyond A.W. Way campground until I came upon the white sign with blue lettering. I turned right onto a gravel driveway and parked under a shady tree.

Lost Coast Blueberries is a certified organic farm. The Mattoles purchased it in 1999. Mattole (the man on the phone) and his wife Jeanne Mattole moved from Oregon to live by the Mattole River. They had lived on the river when they had property in Ettersburg in the '70s and '80s, and were wanting to return to the river. The blueberry farm offered them the chance.

There are three kinds of berries - Spartan, Earliblue and Nelson, the Nelsons being the tartest. Those were in the backyard so I just picked the other two from rows of bushes under protective bird netting. I was in awe at the abundance of berries on the bushes which were full and nearly 7 feet tall - bigger than the bushes at Wolfsen's Farm. (I wouldn't say that the taste of one organic blueberry farm's berries was better than the other, just the setting in Honeydew is much prettier.) One bush easily provided a basketful. I filled five baskets, paid my $10 to the honor system jar, then spoke to Jeanne on her porch while her St. Bernard snored like a bull underneath.

Jeanne doesn't claim to be much of a farmer, or baker for that matter, more of a weed abater and composter. Her six grown children helped out the first summer they bought the farm, and summers since, putting up the bird netting and such. The sprinklers are now on computer timers, so Jeanne concentrates on pulling weeds. This past year she used organic fertilizer which improved the output of the bushes. The family used to sell the berries at farmers markets and stores, but "the berries had to be perfect and it was a lot of work." Jeanne is content to let people come and pick their own berries. "If they pick an imperfect one, it doesn't make a difference to me. I still get paid."

Jeanne gave me a copy of a blueberry pie recipe her daughter, Morningstar, uses. It would be a perfect ending to a perfect day to bake a fresh blueberry pie.

When I got home, my dog, Sabaka, and my calico, Jemima, sniffed my front tire. I wondered what all the interest was about. I squatted down and heard a hissing noise. Something that looked like a foxtail had punctured the side wall of my tire. I called our neighbor, Glenn, to rescue this damsel in distress, and got a lesson on tire changing. When that was all taken care of, I didn't want to fuss with the pie crust. I remembered Helen had given me a recipe for Pat-in Pastry which is mixed in the pie plate and shaped to the plate with fingers, no rolling pin.

I used that for my single crust then filled it with Morningstar's filling. There was some left when Dan returned from Phoenix. It was too sweet for his taste, but "Praise the Lord" I found a delicious blueberry pie.

Oil Pat-in Pastry

9" single pie crust

2 c. flour
2 tsp. sugar
pinch of salt
2/3 c. oil
3 T. milk (or water)

In a 9" pie plate, mix flour, sugar and salt. In a measuring cup measure oil then add milk and whip. Stir into flour. Mix with a fork until flour absorbs in. Pat in with fingers, making an edge around rim. Bake at 400 degrees for 17-20 minutes.

Note: My first attempt produced a crust that was a bit crumbly versus flaky, but it was convenient.

Morningstar's Blueberry Pie

One 8 or 9" single pie crust, baked

3/4 c. sugar
3 T. corn starch
1/8 tsp. salt
4 c. blueberries
1/4 c. water
1 T. butter
1 T. lemon juice

Bake pie crust. Combine sugar, cornstarch, and salt in medium saucepan. Add 2 cups berries and water. Cook over medium heat, stirring constantly until mixture boils and thickens. Remove and stir in butter and lemon juice. Cool. Place 2 cups fresh berries into pie shell. Pour sauce over berries. Chill and serve cold.

Note: If you like a little more zip, add another teaspoon of lemon juice.

It's Fair Time!

Show me the money!

The Humboldt County Fair happens each year in August. Dan and I try to go every year because you can see exciting things at the fair!

Mule races, pig races, carnie sitings, a chainsaw juggler and (drum roll please) a human cannonball! This stunt guy shot out of a huge red, white and blue cannon, flew 70 feet over the funnel cake vendor and somersaulted into a net. Spectacular!

One year at the fair we even experienced an earthquake.

We were in the Art Building looking at the juried art when the rickety wood building creaked and shook, tilting paintings on the wall. We sprinted out of there faster than a thoroughbred in a quarter-mile race. The ground rippled down the midway sending lemonade in plexiglass tanks sloshing back and forth like wave machines.

Then there are the animal exhibits. We usually check out the bunnies, especially the lop-eared ones. And if we're lucky, we're there on the day they have the dog agility tests. There was one dog who stopped at the top of the incline, posed for the audience, and soaked in the attention like a starlet before continuing down the ramp. We laughed so hard tears ran down our faces.

And the horse races. We love the horse races! Dan always has his private little side bets that he won't reveal until after each race. If we win any money, we get a beer and a corn dog to celebrate.

After the races, we stroll around and people watch while I down a brick of greasy Kurly Fries doused in ketchup, which every year over a belly ache I swear I will never eat again.

I've even entered contests, winning ribbons for photos and art. I won second place for my oatmeal cookies, but I never entered a pie before.

This year, I had a good reason to. I sent my entry form in and signed up for five categories: Single Crust Pies, Apple Pies, Berry Pies, Peach Pies and Any Other 2 Crust Pies.

I was all excited about making Sylvia's Raspberry Pie for the Single Crust entry. Based on the feedback she got from family and friends, and that rarely do you come across pie made with Jell-O, we were sure it was unique - a definite winner. Even though the entry was under my name, it was Sylvia who would get the ribbon. I was merely the matchmaker - pie with judge.

My meager raspberry bushes were past their prime, so Sylvia volunteered to supply the berries. One evening we met at Murphy's Market on Glendale Avenue where she passed off two heaping baskets. I put the berries on a cookie sheet and froze them for the BIG BAKING DAY.

I must have read that fair exhibitor's guide a hundred times. I was paying extra special attention since the Single Crust Pie was due a week earlier than the others. On the Wednesday, August 6 slot in my weekly organizer, I wrote "bring pie to fair," and blocked the day off to any other work or activities.

That morning I woke up with diarrhea.

Between runs to the bathroom, I took the raspberries out to thaw. Then I cooked the single crust. It didn't look good so I made another one which looked worse. I went with the first one. Then I went to the bathroom. Again and again.

After the crust cooled, I gathered the filling ingredients. I didn't have enough raspberry Jell-O, so I ran to Murphy's before my stomach acted up, and got more along with a bucket of Swirl Whip for the topping.

It was afternoon by the time I made the filling and set the pie in the refrigerator to chill. I checked the whipped topping instructions which said to thaw in the refrigerator for five hours. Five hours! My entry needed to be in TODAY. Against package warnings, I set it out on the countertop.

In the meantime, a horrendous backache set in. Kidney infection? How was I going to drive all the way to Ferndale hunched over with a flaming backache and needing to pee every half hour?

Then I thought of Sylvia. Her generosity. Her pride in the recipe. The fact that she picked the berries. I sucked in all the pain, spread the top with whipped cream, packed ice around the pie plate and headed to Ferndale.

A nice security guard led me to Belotti Hall. I found a fair representative and asked her where I should put my food entry. She looked at me kind of funny.

"Aren't you taking food today?" I asked out of breath.

"Ah, not sure, let me ask," she said. She consulted with another fair volunteer who disappeared to the back of the hall. She came back wearing a face looking as if she stepped on a tack, and said, "They judged those last night."

Wasn't today August 7? Yes, but they were due Wednesday, August 6th. Even though I read the exhibitor's guide that morning, I still didn't see I had missed the date. I was more worried about making the best entry out of Sylvia's recipe that I was blinded to the details in front of me.

"It sure looks good," said the fair volunteer with a forced grin. Then seeing that nothing would cheer me up, she uttered , "Sorry."

"It's been a bad day," I moaned.

I lugged the pie back to the car and, with tears of frustration in my eyes, drove to Caltrans to cry on Dan's shoulder. He sent me home feeling better, but not any smarter. He'd bring the pie to work tomorrow when his friends were back in the office.

I got home and called Sylvia to confess my mistake. I detected some disappointment in her voice for her pie not being in the fair, but being the kind person that she is, she consoled me.

"Maybe next year," she said.

"But I wanted to win a ribbon for you, Sylvia. Now the only people going to taste it are my husband's friends at work."

Sylvia said it was just a different panel of judges. And that I didn't need a ribbon. "Hugs and kisses are just as good," she said.

That night Dan had two pieces and declared the flavor had no diminishing rate of return - the highest of compliments. Still, I wondered if it could have been a winner.

The next morning when I opened the refrigerator, a blue ribbon dangled from the pie.

ROUND TWO.

The next batch of pies were due on Tuesday, August 12. Really. I quadruple checked. This time I started making them a day ahead. But why should that guarantee that everything would go smoothly?

First of all, the peaches purchased at a stand in Willow Creek on Saturday still were not ripe. The fruit stand man warned me that there might be brown rot due to the recent thunderstorms. Sure enough, they were rotting, but why weren't they ripening? I made the Peach 'n Blueberry Pie anyway and cut the salvageable peaches real thin. The only bad thing about this contest is you can't cut a slice of your pie to sample it before entering it. How would I know how the peaches turned out? I decided to let the hard peaches sit all day in the sun before I made my Peach Rum Pie.

Onto the Strawberry Pie. Rhubarb is what made my last strawberry pie taste best, but this was the Berry Pie category, so rhubarb doesn't count. Plain strawberry needed something to spruce it up - a lattice top!

It turned out a little overdone on the crust, but the red of the strawberry showing through the lattice looked pretty. I wondered about the taste and texture since the strawberries were previously frozen. Fresh would have been better.

Next up - apple pie. I wanted to use Fieldbrook Valley Apple Farms apples but they weren't ready for market so I shopped at Ray's and bought a variety: Granny Smith, Fuji and Braeburn. I was going with the mixed-is-better theory.

I could tell just by the smell of the filling that this pie was going to turn out fabulously. The crust was a beautiful brown, not much filling oozed out, and it had that wonderful smell of apples and cinnamon - the smell of crisp autumn days. I had a good feeling about this one.

By this time it was late afternoon and all I had done was bake three pies. One more to go. I checked the peaches set out on the deck. Still not ripe. Just covered with ants. I cleaned them up and made the decision to let them sit overnight. Inside.

The next morning, the brown spots were more abundant and some were molding! But the peaches still were not ripe or sweet. I went to the grocery store to see if there were any ripe peaches. None. All hard as rocks. I had no choice. I had to make that pie.

I cut the rot off and sliced the peaches super thin. When the slices were mixed with the sugar for the filling, they got juicier and actually let off a faint sweet smell. I splashed some dark rum in the mixture as a christening, and prayed the peaches would cook up sweet.

One bright spot in this whole ordeal was that I found a crust recipe that worked under pressure - the No Fail Pie Crust from Sylvia, only I used regular Crisco instead of butter flavored. The apple cider put off an intoxicating aroma and the pliability of the dough was perfect. No cracking.

I carefully packed the four pies in the SUV and drove to Ferndale, nearly rear-ending a woman who suddenly changed lanes. All the while I wondered who I'd be up against in the competition. I was certain there was a group of elderly Ferndale ladies who had an upper hand just by the fact that they lived in farm country and had years of experience over me. Or what about those professional fair entrants? The ones who won ribbons year after year for making jams, decorating cakes, sewing quilts? What if they decided to make the pie category their focus? A microwave oven for the most overall points was enticement enough. We needed a new microwave oven and for a split second, I thought, what if I won an oven?

Who was I kidding? By the time I reached Ferndale I was resigned to winning the third place overall prize of $25 cash. At least I could recoup some of my grocery costs.

I made it to the fair grounds with a half hour to spare before the deadline. Like a tight end making his way to the end zone, I slipped past the curious parking attendant at the scrimmage line, dashed toward the front gate, deflected a one-two block of drooling security guards, and managed not to trip over the electrical cords powering the kettle corn booth. I plunked the four pies on the registration table and sighed. It was now in the hands of the judges.

I wasn't able to get back to the fair to see if I had won anything, but our friends, the Birds, whom we were camping with that weekend, were heading down on Friday to see their daughter, Antonia, perform at Friendship Square.

"If you have time, check in Belotti Hall to see if I won," I asked Gary. "We'll see you at the lookout tonight."

Dan and I had reserved the Bear Basin Butte Lookout Tower for Friday and Saturday nights and invited the Birds. We went last year as guests of the Flannerys and were awestruck by the top-of-the-world views, the tower, the cabin, the clean bathroom - everything! After that trip we vowed to go back. We had spent enough camping trips among the partying, generator-running masses at campsites with outhouses so smelly I would put off going to near bursting, then hold my breath and hope no flies would land on my butt while I was relieving. So the $75 a night fee was justified.

The Birds arrived in a cloud of dust on that dry afternoon. From Eureka they drove down to Ferndale to the fair, scrambled around there for a few hours, then headed north and drove another three hours to get to the lookout. I knew they had gone to the fair solely to see Antonia perform, so I didn't expect Gary to check out the baked goods, and now he was on vacation so I wouldn't press him.

Gary propped himself on the picnic table. "I saw the pies," he said, then paused for dramatic effect.

I was excited to hear the results, yet didn't want to spoil my vacation if it was bad news. Still, I had to know.

"Did you see mine?"

At this moment, Gary had the power of an Academy Award emcee who held the envelope with the winner for Best Picture.

"In the apple pie category," he said, "you won second prize."

Everyone ooo-ed. A ribbon! I had won a ribbon! Proof that I could make a good crust. Let's have a beer.

Gary gave me a twinkly look.

"Then in the berry category you won-" WHAT? THERE'S MORE? "a first place."

I jumped up and down, clapping like a little girl. The strawberry pie with the lattice won!

"And in the other category-" YOU'RE KIDDING "you won a first place."

Wa-hoo! The peach-blueberry combination was a winner!

"And in the peach category-" HUH? "a first place ribbon."

Three first places and a second! It was too good to be true!

128

Then it dawned on me. What if mine was the only entry and the judge felt sorry for me? I gave Gary an inquisition.

"Were there any other entries?"

"I don't know. I was just looking for your pies."

"Did you see any other names?"

"I mostly just saw your name - Natasha Wing, Natasha Wing, Natasha Wing, Natasha Wing."

"Is there anything you're not telling me?"

His brown eyes darted to the right.

"No, no. That's all I saw."

I didn't know if I should be thrilled or feel like a fool.

"Hey," said Gary. "Even if yours was the only entry, that shouldn't diminish the prize."

He was right. It took a lot for me to even get those entries to the fair. That's more than most people did.

Four ribbons. I went to bed that night under a clear sky dreaming of a new microwave oven.

That Monday, after the fair was over, I drove back to the fairgrounds to collect my pie plates. There, in the glass cabinet were my moldy pies with ribbons dangling from them and I couldn't have been more proud.

To top it off, I won a mini-sweeps award of a $25 gift certificate for Safeway.

Just out of curiosity, I asked the fair volunteer how many entries there were in each category. She directed me to the fair office where the official entry books were. A nice woman put her lunch down to help me.

First category she looked up was Apple.

"There was you and Pam," she said. "Pam Mauney, the Ferndale postmaster. I didn't get to taste yours, but Pam's was delicious. Apple Cinnamon. Her crust was outstanding."

Pam had taken Best of Category with her apple pie. Not a bad entry to lose to.

Then came the other categories. The woman flipped through the notebook. In each category, I was the only entrant.

"Don't feel bad about that," she said. "The judges are under no obligation to give out a prize if there is only one entry. They still have to think it's worthy to award a ribbon, and you got first place."

She showed me the comments stapled to the entry tag. "Very nice pie!" "Tasty pie." And my favorite, "Beautiful crust."

I thanked her for taking time out of her lunch then drove to the Ferndale Post Office to find out what's Pam got, that I don't got?

The following recipes have been renamed in honor of winning blue ribbons at the 2003 Humboldt County Fair.

Peach 'n Blue(ribbon)berry Pie

Pastry for two 9" crusts
white of 1 egg
5 ripe peaches, peeled, enough for 2 c.
juice of 2 lemons, divided
2 c. blueberries
2/3 c. granulated sugar
dash of cinnamon and nutmeg
3 T. quick-cooking tapioca
3 T. butter

Preheat oven to 425 degrees. Brush bottom crust with egg white. Prepare peeled whole peaches by poaching for 2 minutes in boiling water. Remove with slotted spoon and place in cold water until cool. Slice and sprinkle with juice from 1 lemon. Combine in a large bowl-peaches, blueberries, juice from 1 lemon, sugar, cinnamon and nutmeg. Stir in tapioca. Pour into crust and dot with butter. Roll out remaining crust. Cut slits and put crust on top. Brush crust with egg white. Bake for 10 minutes, then lower heat to 350 degrees and continue baking for 35-40 minutes.

No Contest Strawberry Pie

Pastry for two 9" crusts
1-1/3 c. sugar
1/3 c. all-purpose flour
4 c. sliced strawberries
2 T. butter

Prepare pastry. Heat oven to 425 degrees. Mix sugar and flour. Turn in strawberries. Dot with butter. With the top crust, cut 1/2" wide strips then weave them into a lattice top. Fold trimmed edge of lower crust over ends of strips. Form a high edge to help prevent juices from overflowing. Bake until crust is brown and juice begins to bubble, about 45 minutes.

First Prize Peach Pie

Pastry for two 9" crusts
1 c. sugar
1/4 c. all-purpose flour
1/4 tsp. cinnamon
5 c. sliced fresh peaches

1 tsp. lemon juice
2 T. butter
splash of dark rum

Prepare pastry. Heat oven to 425 degrees. Mix sugar, flour and cinnamon. Stir in peaches, lemon juice and rum. Dot with butter and cover with top crust that has slits in it. Seal and flute. Brush with mayonnaise. Cover edge with aluminum foil to prevent over browning. Bake for 30 minutes then remove foil and bake for another 15 minutes or until crust is brown and juice bubbles through slits.

Best of Category

Ferndale Postmaster Pam Mauney delivers at the county fair.

Pam Mauney, the Ferndale Postmaster, greeted me with a soft smile. I reached out to shake her hand as if I was meeting a celebrity.

"Hi, I'm Natasha Wing, and I entered the pie contest at the fair."

"Oh, yes, I thought your name sounded familiar. Didn't you enter four pies? That's a lot of pies."

I explained why so many, "but you. You won the Apple pie category and the Best of Category. Congratulations."

She shook it off. "I've never done that before," she admitted.

"The lady at the fair office said yours was the best crust she has ever tasted."

Pam blushed a peachy color.

"You never know if the crust is going to turn out," she said. "It depends on the temperature of the ingredients, how much you work it, the humidity."

"Did you use the vinegar and egg recipe?"

She had. "And I don't use only one kind of apple. I use many kinds. We have an old apple tree in our yard. Been there since the '30s."

Aha! That's what edged me out. She had native-grown apples versus my random mixture from Ray's.

I gave her my card and asked if I could interview her another time when she wasn't working.

It took a while for us to connect, but it was worth the wait.

Pam, 57, grew up in Ferndale and belongs to the Ferndale Garden Club, sings in the Community Choir, and is a member of the Chamber of Commerce. She has been the postmaster in Ferndale since 1995.

"I know all the people in town, and their great grandmoms."

She lives in a 1935 Craftsman home that her husband remodeled. They have one son.

"I like Ferndale. It gives you a good feeling about where you live, that it's safe. We're lucky to be able to do all our business in town. It's all here. The community feeling is nice. People truly care. When something happens, people are right there to help. Everyone is family."

In her backyard is an old apple tree which bears some sort of King-like apples, which are sweet and crisp. They aren't ready until late in the season, way past the August fair deadline, so Pam used some frozen ones from the previous year, then mixed them with Beverly Hills apples, an early ripening blush yellow apple that's also sweet. This combination won her a Best of Category prize.

Pam first started entering the food categories at the fair when she was in her early twenties and newly married. She had entered her grandmother's recipe for coffee buns, pies and butter cookies. Her grandmother was from Denmark and had taught her how to bake.

"My grandmother used to take her friends to the fair to show off her granddaughter's entries."

Pam has been entering the fair contests for the past 25 years or so. This year she submitted 40 entries including canning, pies, cakes, cookies, breads, pickles, not to mention needlework and begonias. Not only did she win Best of Category for pies, but the Fieldbrook Valley Apple Farms prize (third year in a row), the lemon pie prize, numerous first place ribbons, and the creme de la creme - the Exhibitor of the Year. Guess who won the microwave oven?

So that's who I was up against in the apple pie category - a professional exhibitor! No wonder.

"Were there any categories you didn't win?" I asked.

"Yeast breads," said Pam. "I've never won for my grandmother's coffee buns. Only came in second." Bernice Larson of Fortuna was the fly in the frosting taking first prize.

It was hard enough for me to bake three pies. How did Pam do 40 entries?

"Some of them were jams and jellies and pickles that I can before the fair."

She then paused and softly laughed. "But 40 is a lot. I probably won't do that again. My lemon pie almost slid off the seat on the way down to the fairgrounds."

Gram's Pie Crust

3 c. flour
1-1/2 c. lard (or Crisco)
1 T. vinegar

3 T. ice water
1 egg
1 tsp. salt

Combine flour and salt, work in lard or Crisco with a pastry cutter to the consistency of coarse crumbs. Combine vinegar, water and egg. Beat slightly. Work into flour and Crisco mixture just until combined. Divide in half and roll out on well-floured board working it into a ball. Flatten out and roll out, turning often to the shape of your pie plate. The secret is to handle as little as possible.

Best of Category Apple Pie

6-7 c. sliced tart pie apples
1 c. sugar
2 T. flour

1/2 tsp. cinnamon
1 tsp. nutmeg
1/4 tsp. salt

Combine dry ingredients then fold in apples. Once in pie plate, dot with butter, then roll out pie dough and place on top of pie. Brush top with cream and sprinkle with sugar. Bake at 375 degrees for 1 hour, watching carefully and using wet cloth strips around edge of crust (Pam uses an old flour sack dish towel).

Apron Strings

Janice wears her grandma's apron when she bakes pies.

On Saturdays on the Arcata Plaza, farmers market is the hopping place to be. In the height of the season, booths encircle the entire plaza. Musicians and oddballs provide background entertainment while the main attraction, the colorful fruits, flowers and veggies put on a show of their own.

It was on one of these Saturday mornings in August that I accompanied Janice and Jerry Peterson to buy peaches. Nothing beats a ripe, slurpy peach that spills juice down your chin.

Between traveling, his-and-hers families, work and life, Janice wasn't sure when she'd have time to make a peach pie, but wanted to get the peaches while they were in season.

"Still," she said, "a pie made out of frozen fresh peaches beats any peaches you buy in a can." Her plan was to process the peaches, bag them with sugar, freeze the bags, and make pies when she was less busy. Her husband loves the smell of peach pie on a cold winter day.

We found a vendor on the north side of the Plaza who was hawking peaches. As I stood behind Janice in line, I wasn't sure whether to get the gargantuan, giant gargantuan or ridiculously gargantuan ones. Janice leaned back and said, "Get the biggest ones. I'd rather peel less big ones than more little ones, and you don't notice any taste difference." Sold at $22 a lug.

We circled around the Plaza with our lugs of peaches, passing boxes of zucchini and squash, baskets full of yellow, orange and red tomatoes, piles of eggplant, you name it - it seemed as if every vegetable and fruit had reached its peak this week.

We parted hoping for a day soon that we could get together. Janice and I have this telepathic thing where if we go too long without seeing each other, we just think of the other person and she will call. Our conversations usually start off with, "Hey! I was just thinking of you."

Janice is one of the first women I met when Dan and I moved to Humboldt County about 16 years ago. Dan worked with her then husband, so we all met for dinner at Larrupin's when it used to be in Westhaven. I instantly liked Janice - she was sweet with a biting sense of humor, and one of the prettiest, hippest silver-haired ladies I knew. (Wasn't too crazy about the husband, but he's out of the picture). We've been friends since that day.

One thing I admire about Janice is that she went to college later in life, excelled in her classes, and graduated with honors and a boost of new confidence. She is now a social worker at Mad River Adult Day Healthcare, part of the reason for her busyness.

We were able to find a Friday morning to meet between a firewood delivery and a trip to the mall with her granddaughter.

When I arrived at her 1893 Victorian in Arcata, which at one time served as Dr. Horel's Sanitorium, Janice was wearing her grandmother's apron. It was faded pink with tiny flowers and trimmed in black bric-a-brac.

Janice had already measured most of the ingredients and set them around the kitchen table. The peaches sat in a bowl, skinned and shining with juice. I felt like I had stepped onto a set of a photo shoot.

Janice reminisced about her grandmother while she made the crust. "She looked like Mrs. Claus, fat and jolly with rosy cheeks. Extremely ticklish, too."

Janice learned how to make pies by watching her grandmother who used a big wooden rolling pin, dented and stained with berry juice, to roll out her crusts. Grandpa and the kids clamored for her leftover crusts sprinkled with cinnamon and sugar.

"Grandma Jeffries was the best grandma. Never got mad at us. She always had cookies in the cookie jar. When we made popcorn balls, she had a huge metal dish she made them in. Her and I would scoop out what was left in the bowl and ummm."

Janice and her brothers and sisters used to stay over at grandma's house on Saturday nights then go to church with her on Sundays.

Grandma and Grandpa had lots of property on the top of a hill in Oregon where they grew strawberries, raspberries and blackberries for the canneries. They also raised cows from which Grandma made really good minced meat from the meat from the cows' necks.

At the end of strawberry season she'd let the three girls look through the Sears and Montgomery Ward catalogs and pick out any dress they wanted.

"My grandma always wore house dresses, ironed and starched, even when she was working in the fields. She was fat so she used to make short apron strings and just pin them to her dresses."

Janice finds comfort in wearing her grandmother's apron when she bakes.

"I like to think she's with me when I bake pies."

Grandma Jeffries's Crust

Makes two 9" pie crusts

2 c. flour
2/3 c. + 3 T. Crisco
1/4 c. water
Note: Janice tries to keep the dough sticky by adding more
water if necessary.

Grandma Jeffries's Peach Pie

5 c. sliced peaches, skins removed
3/4 c. brown sugar
2 T. flour or tapioca
3/4 tsp. cinnamon
1/4 tsp. nutmeg
sprinkle of powdered ginger
1/4 tsp. salt
1 T. lemon juice
2 drops almond extract
2 T. butter

Combine sugar, flour, spices, and salt. Add sliced peaches
and mix. Add lemon juice and almond extract. Pour into
pie shell. Dot with butter. Put top crust on and crimp.
Prick with a fork. Sprinkle top with white sugar. Bake at
400 degrees for 15 minutes then turn down to 300 degrees and bake for another 45 to 50 minutes.
Janice's tip for an easy lattice top design: Instead of weav-
ing the dough strips, twist them.

How to Remove Peach Skins

1. Fill a big pot half full with water and bring to a boil.

2. Dip peaches in boiling water for about a minute. Dip the peaches in cold water.

3. Drain peaches, and with your thumbs, push on skin. It should slip off. (Another way to get the process started is to make a cut in the skin, then work it off with your thumbs.)

4. Cut peach in half and remove the pit.

5. Slice for pie filling.

Invasion of the Berry Snatchers

Gina makes Himalayan pies from berries picked in her backyard.

All over Humboldt County, vagrants, RVers, kids on bikes, joggers and HSU students are stopping along roadsides with buckets and sticks.

Beware! It's the invasion of the berry snatchers!

While many Humboldt County natives turn their noses up at Himalayans, many of us relocated residents can't believe how abundant they are! We eagerly pick them for pies, jellies and jams, even stepping around bear skat and risking scraped arms to do so.

Gina Pierce is a berry snatcher.

Gina moved to Humboldt County from Chico 16 years ago. She and her husband, Robin, packed their three kids and dog in a van and headed to the coast so that Robin could go back to school. He had been to Humboldt County on bus trips, and loved the area. A landlord steered them toward looking for a place in Fieldbrook since they were used to a hot, sunny climate.

Their first rental was in Fieldbrook, in a small house where the landlord told them if they took down the shed, they could have two weeks of rent free. The family has lived in Fieldbrook ever since, finding a nice flat piece of property to sustain their vegetable garden and honking geese.

Now that her husband is done with school and onto his career, and the boys are grown up, Gina has gone back to school. She's taking business classes at HSU.

Gina used to work in the health care industry, and when things got a little stressful, she'd come home, put the coffee can bucket around her neck, and head out to the Himalayan bushes.

"Picking is therapeutic to me," said Gina. "I can turn my mind off and just use my hands."

Robin devised a container that keeps both her hands free to pick. He punched holes on either side of a large coffee can (which holds enough berries for two pies) and clipped a strap in the holes.

"Yard sales are great for finding straps off of old purses," said Gina. "They already have clips on them so you just clip them on the can."

She showed me a few picking cans in the garage and slipped one around her neck for demonstration. It hung at the perfect belly height. She has found jelly jars at yard sales, too, which now lined several shelves in her garage.

People have told me over and over again when making pie dough, not to handle it much. It wasn't until I talked with Gina about how she makes her dough that the message finally sunk in.

"You know how with bread you want to knead it and work it," said Gina, massaging imaginary bread dough. "With pie crust you don't. Leave it alone."

Gina has some tricks on how to not touch the dough. First of all, instead of knives or a dough cutter, she uses an egg whip to blend the shortening with the flour.

"The motion is better on my wrists," said Gina. "I just work a little bit of flour in at a time. And if the dough gets wadded up in the middle of the whip, I just use a knife to get it out."

Once the shortening and flour are blended and water added, Gina uses the back of a spoon to push the dough together.

"I do little pushes all over. When it looks like it's sticking good, I pick it up and make a ball."

"What about all the flour that's left on the bottom of the bowl?" I asked. I always try to stick it onto the ball and work it in. My New England frugalness hates waste.

"Forget about it," said Gina. "You know how you always have a little bit of crust that you have to cut off anyway? There's no need for the flour left in the bowl."

Gina does have a use for that leftover crust, however. She rolls it out flat, spreads it with softened butter, then shakes on cinnamon and sugar. (She keeps cinnamon and sugar premixed in a shaker.) After the pies are out of the oven, she turns the temperature down to 350 and bakes them for 12 minutes.

"My son likes the crust the best anyway."

Gina has even made turnovers by rolling out crust circles, putting leftover filling in the center, then folding the edges and sealing them like a turnover.

As we ate a wonderful slice of her Himalayan pie with vanilla ice cream, I thought the tartness was just right. I loved the cinnamon and sugar sprinkling on top for both looks and taste. And for Pete's sake, the filling didn't taste seedy at all! No toothpicks necessary.

If you have husbands like ours who can't wait for pies to cool, tip and stabilize the pie plate, with the missing slice at the top of the incline, so the juices don't run out and can still set up.

When it comes to native blackberries versus Himalayans, take a tip from Gina and don't be picky. Make the best of what's out your back door, in her case, literally. Looming outside her sliding glass door off the kitchen were Himalayan bushes poised like some alien creature that was about to engulf the house.

Eat them before they eat you!

Himalayan Blackberry Pie

2 crust pie dough

4 c. Himalayan blackberries
1/2 c. flour
1-1/2 to 2 c. sugar (depending on if you prefer tart or sweet)
1 T. butter
cinnamon sugar

Preheat oven to 425 degrees. Mix berries, flour, sugar and set aside. Roll bottom crust and place in pie dish. Place berries in pie dish and put three dots of butter in center. Top with top crust and seal edges.

Place aluminum foil around edges of crust (2" strips) and sprinkle top crust lightly with cinnamon sugar. Bake 40 minutes, removing foil the last 15 minutes of baking. Cool.

Invasive vs. Native

The Himalaya blackberry (*Rubus discolor*) was introduced to North America by Luther Burbank. He called it the Himalayan Giant thinking it was of Asian origin, but it's actually from Europe. Even though he was wrong, the common name, Himalayan blackberry, stuck like thorns. Thanks to Luther and the birds, Himalayan blackberries have become invasive in Humboldt County. Their denseness is a problem because the bushes choke out native plants.

The way to tell a Himalayan blackberry from the native California blackberry (*Rubus ursinus*) is that Himalayans have five leaflets, each toothed and oval shaped. The California blackberry only has three leaflets.

The Himalayan berry is also larger, juicier and seedier - that's why people prefer them for jams, not pies. The native blackberries tend to come into season earlier than Himalayans as well.

According to the Humboldt County Agricultural Center, these native berries can be collected and used for pie-baking.

California blackberry (*Rubus ursinus*)
California huckleberry (*Vaccinium ovatum*)
Salmonberry (*Rubus spectabilis*)
Thimbleberry (*Rubus parviflorus*)
Blackcap raspberry (*Rubus leucodermis*)
Beach strawberry (*Fragaria chiloensis*)
Wood strawberry (*Fragaria vesca*)

Barrie's Berry Pie

Barrie, one of my taste testers, attempts a pie.

Barrie finally got up the nerve to try to make a pie.

Wade's 9-year-old freckly daughter, Amy, was in town staying with them, and Barrie was looking for something they could do together. The Himalayans were ripe - and free - so we picked eight cups of berries along the roadside.

To make things simple, I brought Sylvia's No Fail Pie Crust recipe and Gina's Himalayan pie recipe.

We made the fillings first. As I read off the ingredients, Barrie measured them out. She stirred the berries into the sugar and flour mixture and already you could see they were very juicy.

Right off the bat we didn't have enough Crisco for the crust, so we cut in 3/4 cup of butter, hoping that wouldn't mess things up. After all, it was Barrie's first crust and I wanted the experience to be pleasurable and not give her a chance to say, "See! That's why I don't make them from scratch!"

Then we added the water, apple cider and an egg laid by one of her chickens. Barrie proudly showed me the egg carton that contained five fresh eggs.

"They're finally laying," she said.

Barrie's son, Wendell, wanted chickens, so they raised four from chicks. Wendell named them after the Osbournes - Ozzy, Sharon, Jack and Kelly. I watched the chickens grow from cute little fuzz balls to plump, feathered poop machines. It seemed like it took a long time until they began laying eggs, but the payoff was worth it. Unlike the eggs at grocery stores that have runny whites and pale yolks, fresh eggs had firm whites and an intense deep yellow yolk.

I was kind of concerned how the dough was coming together because of the butter, but it sure was a pretty yellow color. The smell was fabulous, too. Butter mixed with apple cider. Be still my drooling taste buds.

I meant to let Barrie do the rolling out part, but instead my teacher mode took over. Barrie and Amy watched intently while I flattened the dough out. Unfortunately it cracked a lot and was dry so it was with much difficulty and patching that we got the crust into the pie plates.

Barrie poured the berry filling in, then topped it and crimped the edges. She did the honors of adorning the top with venting slits and into the oven it went. We cooked it extra long so that Wade would have his crunchy crust.

Hip-hip hooray! She'd made her first pie from scratch!

I talked to her after I got back from a trip to Tahoe. Dan and I met friends from Southern California there to go mountain bike riding and hiking.

"So?" I asked Barrie. "How did your pie turn out?"

"Aaa," said Barrie. "It was runny." She tried to inject enthusiasm. "Okay I guess. Wade and John liked it. But I kept spitting out seeds, p-tew, p-tew."

Barrie's first attempt was short of spectacular. I hoped this wouldn't keep her from trying again.

At least she partially broke the voodoo spell.

Update...

The spell is broken!

Barrie is now working as a backup baker at Toni's #1, making of all things, pies!

Toni's is a 24-hour restaurant that has been in business for 27 years. Each week they bake about 20 to 25 pies and sell them whole or by the slice.

The morning I went to see Barrie in action, she and the main baker, Jane, had finished making an apple crumb , a cherry crumb, and a marionberry pie. The lemon meringue pie sat on the counter awaiting its meringue topping.

Barrie whipped up a frothy bowl of meringue and Jane showed her how to spread it on just right. She made sure the meringue touched the edge of the crust, then made peaks by taking the flat side of a spatula and lightly spanking the meringue. The little peaks browned up wonderfully.

Jane said, "When I first started here, I couldn't roll out a round crust. But Barrie did great!"

Toni's Key Lime Pie

1 graham cracker crust
1 egg
1 14 oz. can sweetened condensed milk
1/2 cup lime juice (3 limes)
1 12 oz. tub of Cool Whip
dab of green food coloring

Brush graham cracker crust with egg white. Cook about 6 minutes in 350 degree oven. Cool.
Whip condensed milk with food coloring until airy. Fold in Cool Whip. Fold in lime juice. Spread into pie shell and refrigerate.

Note: I made this with an 8" crust and found that an 8 oz. tub of Cool Whip was plenty.

Pickin' and a-Grinnin'

Dorothy finds a new use for a curtain rod.

I made the delicious mistake of going to the Westhaven Blackberry Festival a half hour too early, before the festival had officially begun. Vendors were still gussying up their booths, and strings of colorful plastic flags were being hung to mark the territory. I poked around looking for Florence Couch and found her inside Firemen's Hall, sitting in a chair, rubbing her legs.

"I've been on my feet constantly for two weeks," said Florence, her rosy cheeks flushed, setting off her vivid blue eyes. "Our ovens went out on us while we were trying to get the pies baked."

An army of plastic bags containing baked pies lined three rows of tables, ready to be called to service.

"Did you see the article in the paper?" I asked her. The Times-Standard graciously ran an article I wrote about the upcoming festival and included a photo of the assembly line of pie makers.

"That was good," said Florence, "but I didn't expect the part about me being 81 to be in there," she said with a smile. "Hey, this hair is natural and I earned every one of these grays."

She slowly stood up and asked what she could get me.

"Are you selling the pies yet?" I asked.

"We've been selling them since 8:30."

"How about two frozen blackberry pies and one mixed then."

She came back with the pies and another woman took my $33 check and put the pies into paper bags. Florence had told me that in years past they've had people come in and steal pies, so now they put them in paper bags to know which ones were paid for.

I left the festival before it even got into full swing, but like a criminal, I felt like I left with all the loot since I was one of the lucky ones to get a wild blackberry pie before they were sold out.

Since it was beautiful out, I decided to go north a bit and hike Trinidad Head. There's a semi-easy trail that loops around the head where you can get views of the ocean, beach, and Trinidad, a small fishing village that perches on a bluff and spills down to Trinidad Bay. That morning, the sea lions were barking madly, buoys were clanging, and boats were humming out to sea.

Passing little bunnies munching on grass, and sidestepping a racer-back snake, I completed the loop and headed to Katy's Smokehouse to pick up some smoked salmon for lunch. I mentioned to Judy who worked behind the counter that I had just gone to the Blackberry Festival and that I was working on a book about Humboldt County pie bakers.

"Oh, you need to talk to Dorothy Cox then," she said without hesitation. "My husband loves her pies. She can come home from work and just whip up a pie in no time."

I called Dorothy who lives on Ocean Avenue in Trinidad. Fishing is a main industry here and in June the town holds its annual Fish Festival. When I had called her, she had just taken out a huckleberry pie she was baking for her husband's fishing friend. Berry juice was still bubbling from the crust and spilling onto her countertop.

"I don't eat berries, but I pick them like a crazy woman. Although I won't pick Himalayans to save my life! People tell me they taste good, but I tell them, yeah, if you can get past the seeds!"

I had to meet the lady who picks berries but doesn't eat them. The idea of it just baffled me. Why would something you don't like be so fascinating yet not be the least bit tempting to try? It's like a fox who steals chicken eggs for fun.

Loving a mystery, I visited Dorothy at her house on a grey, drizzly Monday. She and her husband, Dan, raised two boys here. Dan is a commercial crab fisherman and has been fishing for more than 30 years. In the summers he logs.

"Fishing and logging - he's a true Humboldt County worker," chimed Dorothy, swatting him away from the pies on the counter.

Dorothy works as a secretary at Dow's Prairie School in McKinleyville.

"The people I work with, and how the parents get involved

164

there is, well, it's like family."

She's a big fan of football. Her husband played in high school where they met, and her sons played for McKinleyville High. She also loves basketball and follows the high school and Humboldt State teams.

I found myself wishing I either knew shorthand or could cast a Harry Potter spell on my pen to write at super speed since Dorothy had a lot to say - and fast!

"I just love to pick," said Dorothy. "I went yesterday while Danny was out fishing and picked blackberries for four and a half hours."

"When did this addiction start?" I asked in good fun.

"My mom and aunt took me berry picking in Fieldbrook when I was a kid. We'd take a picnic and pick for hours. I couldn't tell you exactly where, but I remember the old barn."

"Did you ever eat the berries?"

"No, I didn't like them."

"Did you eat the pies your mom made with the berries you picked?"

"No."

She ticks off on her fingers, "I'll eat lemon meringue, pumpkin, coconut or chocolate, but not berry."

"Then what is it about picking berries if you don't eat them?"

"It's like meditation for me."

Mystery solved.

Dorothy has secret spots she goes to pick and prefers to go alone. She has been picking so long now that she can scan a patch and tell by its leaves and color if there are ripe berries or not. She even has a special tool she brings along to hook and lift the branches - a curtain rod.

"I can go into a patch where there are pathways of trampled bushes, and I can lift branches and find ripe berries that people have overlooked. But there's nothing worse then going to a patch and seeing red berries, knowing someone got there ahead of you."

It's a well-known fact among her friends that she's an avid picker, so they pass on information about new spots, or ask her to come pick their bushes if they don't have time to get to them themselves. Blackberries pickers generally don't like to reveal their picking spots since they are dwindling due to development. A few goating friends and her nephew, Lars, have been reluctantly asked along to pick, but "I like it better when they don't talk and are off a ways," she said, laughing at her silliness.

Her husband is on the lookout for patches, too. Sometimes he'll pull over to the side of the road and whip out his binoculars to scope out an area.

Dorothy showed me her purple stained fingers with dark lines under her nails.

"I have a free manicure coming and I'm trying to figure out when I can use it," she said. "Can't during blackberry season, can't during huckleberry season. Peeling apples turns my fingers brown. Guess I'll get my nails done about Christmas!"

If she's not picking in the wild, she often runs out to her mother's house in Willow Creek and picks her nectar berries, marionberries, raspberries and apples. At 88 years old, her mother can't roll crusts out anymore so Dorothy will make crusts for her.

"Every time I make crusts for my mom she'll call me and tell me 'girls your age don't make crusts anymore. They just go out and buy them.'"

Okay, so the burning question: If Dorothy picks obsessively, but doesn't eat the berries, what does she do with the billions of berries she bags?

She showed me her freezer, which was so stuffed with bags of berries they were practically tumbling out; her refrigerator, which had more bags of berries waiting to become pies; and pointed to the garage where a deep freezer was full of berry bags.

"I don't give berries away. I'll make pies and cobblers and give those away." She has one neighbor who, when he finds out she has a pie for him, will come up the street right away to collect. For school potlucks she brings a giant pan of cobbler. She's always giving a slice away here and there.

There is a new spot Dorothy discovered the other day, where wild blackberries grow. All I can say is it's in McKinleyville. Her brown eyes glazed over at the thought of it, and she was practically drooling thinking of the number she had seen. She was champing at the bit to go back. I asked if I could come along. She hesitated then wiped the countertop with her hand.

I promised I wouldn't talk, or give up the spot location.

"I, yeah, you can come along. Someone else told me about this spot and there were other people there, so yeah, that would be okay."

She was feeling the back-to-work crunch and tried to figure out when she could go next. This afternoon was out. She was making apple sauce.

"School starts up next week. I'll have to put my rod and bucket in the car and go afterwards." She'd call me about when I could come along.

In the meantime, I had some pie to sample, which she had to swat her husband away from several times.

One of Dorothy's favorite pies is one she adapted from a 1952 Betty Crocker cookbook recipe for French Glacé Raspberry Pie. Instead of straining the juices off to make the glacé, she just mashes the raspberries. For the pie she served me that day, she made it in a 10" deep dish glass pie pan, so she doubled the recipe. One of my favorite pies I make uses this recipe (for a 9" regular pie plate) only with strawberries. I add a little cinnamon to my cream cheese. But after tasting the raspberry flavor, I like it better than strawberry. The tart thing, again.

Her husband's favorite fruit pie is huckleberry. Dorothy took out a little cookbook she bought that was titled "Huckleberries and Crabmeat: Recipes from the Pacific Coast" compiled by Carol Cate.

"I thought it was funny how it combined both of us," said Dorothy, nodding to Danny.

On page 93 I found an intriguing recipe for Huckleberry Pot Pie, another bottomless pie. When I made this recipe I substituted blueberries for the huckleberries and maple syrup for the maple sugar. My hubby said it was FANTASTIC, and he's not a blueberry lover.

I heard from Dorothy a few weeks later. She had started back to work and was busy, busy, busy, and I had just gotten back from camping. We finally connected.

"Meet me behind the -- ," said Dorothy. (Nuh-ah, I promised not to reveal)

I was curious to see how her tool worked. Dorothy put on an

old, long-sleeved button down men's shirt. With curtain rod in one hand and container in another, she led me down a path. The curtain rod turned out to be a weapon as well as a tool as Dorothy relentlessly slashed at Himalayan bush runners.

"Uck, get out of the way," she said. "You don't want these." She picked a Himalayan and worked it around in her mouth and made a sour face. "Seeds, blah."

Then she stooped down and showed me the wild blackberry vines intertwined with the Himalayans. She pulled a vine closer with her curtain rod.

"See, the thorns are smaller and closer together. And look. The Himalayan's are big and further apart." She showed me a ripe Himalayan. "These are bigger and just by looking at them they look seedy. Here's a blackberry. Not as big, and compact."

I pointed out that Himalayans have five leaves where blackberries only have three.

"I go by the thorns," she said. "Just something I've learned to spot."

For some reason I thought wild blackberry bushes grew closer to the ground and in different soil than Himalayans, but now I know to look closer at the vines. Unfortunately the wild blackberries were at the tail end of their season and the Himalayans were taking over.

"We'll go next year," said Dorothy. "I'll show you where there's a ton of them."

So my wild blackberry pie would have to wait until next year. Again, it alludes me, but I'm closing in on the wily berry.

But the end of one season only means the beginning of another.

"Huckleberries are coming in early," said Dorothy. "I saw them where my husband was logging. And I've got to go pick raspberries. The second season is here."

She paused and grinned in defeat. "I'm obsessed," she confessed giving me a what-can-you-do shrug.

French Glacé Raspberry Pie

One 10" pie crust
2 qt. raspberries
6 oz. of softened cream cheese
2 c. sugar
6 T. cornstarch

Bake 10" pie crust (Dorothy uses Butter flavor Crisco recipe). Spread cream cheese over bottom of cooled shell. Cover with half of berries. Mash the rest of the berries. Bring to boil and mix into sugar and cornstarch mix. Cook over low heat, stirring constantly, until boiling. Boil 1 minute. Cool. Pour over berries in pie shell. Chill 2 hours. Top with whipped cream.

Huckleberry Pot Pie

Reprinted with author Carol Cate's permission from "Huckleberries and Crabmeat: Recipes from the Pacific Coast."

1 c. sugar
1/2 tsp. cinnamon
1/4 tsp. nutmeg
3-1/2 T. flour
2 T. maple sugar
1/4 tsp. salt

4 c. huckleberries
2 T. lemon juice
2 T. butter
unbaked pastry
1 tsp. milk

Butter a baking dish. Mix dry ingredients together. Blend lightly with huckleberries. Put into baking dish. Pour lemon juice over all and dot with butter. Cover with pastry. Make a fluted rim. Cut slices in top with a sharp knife. Brush with milk. Bake 400 degrees - 40 minutes.

Four and Twenty Black Birds

Sing, pie bird, sing!

Carol gave me an antique pie vent from England shaped like a black bird for Christmas. It sits on my window sill over my kitchen sink, its beak open, poised to let off steam at a moment's notice.

Pie birds were invented in England in the early 1800s by bakers who were tired of the juices bubbling out and making a black mess of their ovens.

I tried using the pie bird. Once.

I made a Himalayan pie then shoved the bird into the center of the top crust. It stuck way out. When the pie was cooked, I pulled the pie bird out leaving a gaping hole in the middle that wasn't very attractive. I thought a pie bird was a dumb idea -slits worked just fine - and never used it again.

Until I learned how to actually use a pie bird. Pie birds, or pie funnels as they are called in England, vent steam that builds up in pies so the juices don't bubble over. They also keep the crust from sagging. At first they were functional, a funnel shape made of glass or ceramic. In the 1920s they became whimsical figurines.

The way it works is there is a hole, or arch, in the sides of the figure's base and a smaller one at the top to allow steam to escape.

Apparently you're supposed to line the pie plate with the pastry then place the bird in the center. You pour the filling in around the bird, cut an X in the center of the top crust and slip it over the bird's head. Then you push the crust around the bird's shoulders so that just the head sticks out. And you don't yank it out when the pie is done. Now that made more sense.

When Dan and I went to Kansas City for his 30th high school reunion, we went to an antique show. One dealer who travels to England had ceramic pie funnels for only $4.50. I bought one and sat it on the sill next to my pie bird.

Now if only someone could invent a funnel to stick in our heads when we need to let off a little steam...

Mom's Apple Pie

My Mom.

When I ask people about their memories of pie, many remember their moms baking apple pies. I don't.

I claim to not have a good memory of my childhood, that is until I get together with my younger sister, Nina, who has an incredible memory, and then it all starts flowing again. I emailed my mom and asked if she used to bake pies for us as kids. She emailed back that she used to make cakes and pies for us "all the time."

Hence the sweet tooth and thighs.

As a kid I preferred cake over pies (it's a frosting thing), so that's the reason for the mind block I'm sure. My mom used to make cakes in different shapes before themed birthday parties were cool. Since my birthday is a week before Valentine's day I used to get heart-shaped cakes. She'd bake a square cake and a round one, then cut the round one in half, turn the square on a point to make a diamond shape, and cleverly use the half-circles to make a heart. Then she'd frost it in thick pink frosting tinted with cherry juice. It was yummy.

Now that I'm grown up, I prefer pies. It's a fruit thing.

One little secret I have when making apple pies is that instead of using white sugar, I use raw cane sugar. It seems to infuse an old-fashioned taste into the filling.

Here's another tip. After slicing apples for hours by hand one time to make apple sauce with my friend, Tauni, her brother, practical one that he is, asked why we didn't use apple slicers.

"Seems to me a quick crank takes a whole lot less time than doing it by hand," he said as he passed through the kitchen. We glared at him, our fingers sore and our wrists aching with carpal tunnel. In our hearts we wanted to do it the way women in the past did. And we were convinced that the love we put into hand peeling the apples is what made the apple sauce taste so wonderful that I ate a jarful before it even cooled. But one day shortly after that, I got a call from Tauni saying she picked up an apple slicer on sale at the mall and it liberated her from hours of slicing. Apple sauce tasted the same, too, she said. So I ran down to the store and got one for myself and have been praising the inventor ever since. Pare, slice and core all in one crank. A modern marvel!

So now when I make apple pies I don't get that "Oh God, it's going to take FOREVER to make one" feeling. I actually look forward to using my peeler.

When I got Mom's recipe and she mentioned that she mounds the apples up, the memories of her apple pies flooded back. I remembered being so mesmerized by the mountain of apples and amazed at how she was able to stretch the top crust over them.

Then I realized that I stack my apples, too. Must be hereditary.

No Fail Pastry Shells

From Mom's 1958 Betty Crocker cook book

For a two crust pie:
2 c. of sifted Gold Medal flour
1 1/2 tsp. salt
1/2 c. cooking oil (canola or vegetable)
1/4 c. cold milk

Mix flour and salt. Pour oil and milk all at the same time into the flour and salt mix. Stir with a fork until mixed. Dough looks moist, but isn't sticky. Press into a ball and cut in half, flatten halves slightly. Place one half between 2 sheets of wax paper (12 inch square). Roll out gently to edges of the paper. Dampen countertop very slightly to prevent paper from slipping while rolling. Peel off top paper. If dough tears press together without moistening. Lift paper and pastry by top corners. Place paper- side-up in pie pan. Remove paper. Add filling. Trim crust even with rim. Repeat the process for the top crust. Place over filling and remove paper. Press rim together with the tongs of a dinner fork. Makes a pretty pattern. Trim edges. Make very small slices in the top of the crust to let steam out while baking.

This is a recipe Mom made up for apple pie. I asked her how many apples and she said she doesn't measure, just mounds. So I'm guessing 6 to 8? Maybe more.

Mom's Apple Pie

6-8 apples
1 c. plus 2 T. sugar
1 tsp. cinnamon
1 tsp. nutmeg
1 T. flour
1 T. butter

Core and peel apples (preferably hard apples like Granny Smith or Fugi). Slice very thin into bottom pie crust until mounded as high as possible. (Apples will shrink as they cook.) Mix 1 cup of sugar with 1 teaspoon of cinnamon, 1 teaspoon of nutmeg, and 1 tablespoon of flour. Sprinkle over top of apples. Cut about 1 tablespoon of butter in small pieces and place on top of apples. Place top crust on and put small venting slices in the top. Mix 2 tablespoons sugar with a little cinnamon and sprinkle over the top crust.
Temperature: 425 degrees Time: Bake 50 to 60 minutes in middle of the oven.

Variations:
1. Trimmed crust can be rolled out and cut into the shape of an apple or any other shape and placed on the top crust.
2. Top crust can be sliced into 3/4" strips and placed across the top of pie in a lattice design.
3. Use a cinnamon stick for a pie vent.

Lattice Top

Laura Parker weaves a lattice top on her apple pie.

One morning, about 8-ish as I was getting out of the shower, I heard the phone ring. I thought it was my agent in New York returning my call from yesterday, so I ran, dripping wet, and answered the phone.

Thank God I don't have one of those phones with a picture screen or the caller would have hung up!

When the voice on the other end turned out to be Laura Parker, a woman from Arcata I had cold called several days ago, I got a little nervous, like a salesman trying to close a deal. I was afraid that she might have thought my phone message I left about pie-making was a bit looney, so I was surprised she even called back. Still, it's hard to be professional when you're naked. Luckily she didn't know.

Laura was a bit hesitant about me interviewing her. "Really," she said, "my pies aren't that special. I follow recipes." I could tell Laura was suffering from what most younger women suffer from, low pie esteem. "My mother can't believe I still don't know how to make a crust by memory. Even if something has two ingredients, I have to look it up."

"I'd like to see how you decorate your pie crusts," I said. "Your friend, Jo, said you make elegant crusts."

If blushing was a noise, I could hear that she was red right now.

"Well, I do make lattice tops. And sometimes I cut out leaves for my pumpkin pies at Thanksgiving."

"That's more than some good pie bakers would do. You tackled the next level of intimidation in pie making!" She laughed. "Next time you have an inkling to make a pie, let me know and I'll come over."

"How about when I make a peach pie. That's my son's favorite."

Before we hung up she mentioned two other people I could call. More leads.

Peach season came and went so we met during apple season. Laura went to Fieldbrook Valley Apple Farms to purchase freshly picked apples for the demonstration pie. The co-owner said his wife just made a wonderful pie with Golden Supreme and Macintosh apples so that's what Laura bought. The Golden Supreme were yellow and firm so they'd keep their shape, and the Macintosh were a bit softer for cooking down.

The Parkers live in a beautiful new-to-look-old Victorian home in Arcata near the high school. Laura has two children, a 14 year old daughter, Hillary, who's a swimmer and a 16 year old son, Bryce, who's at the stage in life where slow is boring. Fast cars are his passion. Manual, not automatic.

Her husband, Dave, co-owns Life Cycle bike shop which he opened in 1974 with his sister, Lynn, and her husband, Vince. Dave had graduated from Humboldt State University and was working for the forest service. A year into his job his sister asked him if he wanted to open a bike shop. None of them had any experience with bikes other than family bike rides, so Lynn and Vince drove their VW Bug down to a police auction and bought used bikes and parts and taught themselves how to work on bikes. Twenty-nine years later, the shop is still pedaling along, and brother and sister and husband still work together. Laura and Dave met through their interest in cycling, but now that she's a mom of teenagers, she doesn't get in as much riding as she'd like.

Knitting, however, she has found time for. Laura started up a knitting group with friends which she hosts at her home.

"We don't do much knitting," confessed Laura. "It's more the fun of getting together and eating, and talking about our projects. The social aspect."

Stitch and bitch is what my husband calls it, but I could see evidence of knitting projects around the house, so I'm sure Laura did more stitching than bitching.

"I may not look it, but I'm sort of a tense person, so knitting is stress release for me." She noted that knitting has become a stress reliever for women CEOs in high-powered city jobs who make scarves over lunch rather than phone calls. Laura knits sweaters, scarves and socks mostly. She also has a sew shop in McKinleyville where one of the things she makes is Comfort Critters, fleece hot water bottle covers shaped like ladybugs, turtles, and bees which she's been selling at craft shows.

"As a kid I always did things with my hands. Macramé. Leather tooling. I just like handwork. My mom was a homemaker and did a lot of cooking and sewing." Laura turned to me in her rose colored cardigan and said, "You know, it's funny sometimes how you turn out to be like your mom."

Laura's mom loved to bake pies for Laura's dad. Blueberry and cherry.

"She'd hide them in closets so he wouldn't see them and then surprise him after dinner."

For the apple pie Laura was making, she used a trusted crust recipe that she adapted from the January 1992 issue of Bon Appetit Classic Desserts. It contains sour cream which sounded intriguing. At first she only used the crust for apple pies, but now uses it with all her fruit pies.

While the dough was chilling in the refrigerator, Laura peeled the apples with a hand peeler and cut them into thick slices which reminded me of those old-fashioned pies where no two slices were the same size. To the apples she added a half of a lemon. She had a little lemon juicer and a mini cloth strainer that caught the pulp and seeds.

Laura had cool gadgets. Besides the lemon juicer, she had a salt mill that measured out portions of a teaspoon. All you had to do was set it to your measurement and pour out the salt. Her oven also buzzed when it was preheated. And, she has a drying rack for plastic lunch bags.

After the filling was done, Laura slowly swirled flour onto the wooden cutting board, and rolled out the bottom crust. After gingerly placing it in the plate, she slid the apples in, then gently tamped them into place with the center piled higher. For the top crust she made lattice strips, working the wooden cutter as if carefully cutting a piece of fabric. Then she wove the strips, over and under, for a pattern that looked like gingham, and topped it off with a sprinkling of cinnamon and sugar.

"I hope these apples are tart," she said. We both agreed how we preferred tart apples over sweet.

"Where do these ideal images and tastes come from?" I asked.
"From memories? From pictures?"

"I don't know," she said, "but I'm that way with chocolate chip
cookies, too! They can't be too dry, or too flat. They have to be the
right moistness. I finally found a recipe for chocolate chip cookies
that makes them like I like them, and have used that ever since."

While the pie baked, the kids came home from school. Bryce
and I talked cars for a bit, Mustangs, which he said his friends call
girlie cars. I told him that's because when they came out, Ford
marketed the Mustang to women drivers. He said I should check
out the 2005 retro Mustang - a tribute to the 40th anniversary.

Laura wanted to get a retro VW Bus that was coming out.
"Remember those kind with all the windows?"

She had one in her 20s which she traveled around in during her
carefree days and apparently missed - the bus and the days. I admitted I bought the Mustang last year during a mini mid-life crisis.
My first car was a 1967 Mustang. Ivy green. Dan and I had brought
it with us from Phoenix to Eureka, but sold it when we needed
money. I missed my Mustang, but perhaps it was more that I missed
the fun it represented when I was single and dating. When I saw a
'64-1/2 in the newspaper, Barrie and I drove to Orleans to look at
it, and I ended up driving it home. Right after I got my '64-1/2
Mustang, I saw my old '67 cruising on Hwy. 101. It was if my old
pony was welcoming the new one to the pasture.

The oven timer sounded. Hillary waited patiently for her mom
to take the pie out. When Laura pulled it out, it was a golden beauty,
the lattice sprucing up the apple filling like lace on a table top.
Laura poked at the apples, wishing they had cooked down more.
Perhaps thinner slices or different apples would have worked.
Hillary didn't care. She cut into it and ate a thick slice before
heading off to swim practice.

It being 4:30 and not wanting to cut into Parker family time, I
took two slices home. The smell of apples and cinnamon perme-
ated my car, and for the 15 minute drive, I was transported to New
England, my childhood stomping grounds.

After dinner, Dan and I ate our pie with vanilla ice cream. Like Laura, I wished the apples had cooked down more and created a little mushiness between the layers, and were perhaps a little more tart. With apple pies, it's all about the apples. But I thought the crust was excellent. It didn't have a sour cream taste like I thought, but the consistency was light and flaky.

"I think the sour cream's a gimmick," said Dan. "Can't taste it."

I savored my bites, reminiscing about how much I really love fall. Cool nights and warm days. The crispness of apples and the colors of their skins. The smell of cinnamon. The crunch of leaves. Scarecrows and pumpkins.

Hillary said she liked fall fruits best. I had to agree. They taste like home.

Laura's Sour Cream Pie Crust

1/4 c. plus 2 T. sour cream
2 T. ice water
1 tsp. sugar
3/4 tsp. salt
2-1/2 c. flour
1/2 c. unsalted butter, chilled
1/2 c. Crisco, chilled

Combine sour cream, water, sugar and salt in measuring cup. In large bowl, put in flour and cut in butter and shortening with pastry blender until it looks like coarse meal. Add sour cream mixture and stir until dough forms. Don't overdo. Turn dough onto floured surface. Divide in half and form each half into a ball. Flatten into disk and wrap in cellophane. Refrigerate one hour.

Parker-style Apple Pie

Here's the apple pie recipe Laura adapted from Bon Appetit's Dutch-style Apple Pie recipe.

2 Sour Cream Pie Crust Dough disks
8 apples (mixture of Golden Supreme and Macintosh, or your choice) peeled, cored and sliced.
1/2 c. sugar (varies depending on variety of apple)
3 T. all purpose flour
1 tsp. cinnamon
2 T. fresh lemon juice

Preheat oven to 425 degrees. Mix sugar, flour and cinnamon. Add apples and mix. Add lemon juice and mix in. Roll one pie crust disk out on lightly floured cutting board. Put into 9" pie plate. Fill with filling. Roll out other disk and cut into strips, about 1/2" wide. Weave lattice pattern with strips on top of apples. Press lattice ends to bottom crust to seal. Sprinkle with cinnamon and sugar. Bake about 1 hour or until apples are tender and crust is golden brown. Cool until warm. Serve plain or with vanilla ice cream or cream.

Apples and Oranges

Vince at Life Cycle bike shop in Arcata.

Lance Armstrong smiled at me from the cover of his book as I followed Vince Smith through his bike shop to the back room to talk about pie.

"Watch out for grease," he cautioned as I propped myself on a wooden stool. Tools and skeletal parts of bikes hung in the background.

In the summer of 1973, Vince and his wife, Lynn, rode their bikes from Colorado to Massachusetts. It took a month going about 100 miles a day. Along the way they stopped in small towns and bike shops.

"Bike shops?" I asked. "Not monuments or parks?"

"There wasn't much else to do in the mid-West," said Vince.

This trip gave them time to think about what they would do next with their lives. They were tired of the Bay Area. Vince was an elementary school teacher, and when he looked at his fellow co-workers and flashed forward to the future in education, he decided he wanted a more low-key workplace and more control over his life and livelihood. It was during this trip that he and Lynn considered opening a bike shop.

"It seemed like a good life at bike shops."

When they came up to Humboldt County to visit Lynn's brother, Dave Parker, in November 1974, the store at the corner of 16th and G streets in Arcata was empty. On impulse they decided to rent the space. They convinced Dave to leave his forestry job, and while Vince went back to Palo Alto to finish out teaching the school year, Dave and Lynn worked on the store, with Vince helping on weekends when he could. Life Cycle opened in February 1975 and Vince joined them in June.

"At first there was not much business here. But in the long term it proved to be a great place to have a bike shop and business."

Vince laughed at the early days. There were black and white photos of the young entrepreneurs posted in the bike shop.

"I remember we drove Dave's small car down to a wholesaler in the Bay Area and loaded his trunk up with $1,000 dollars of inventory. We set it up in the shop and thought we were ready to go."

Today the shop was loaded with rows of bikes, clothes, racks of accessories and parts, and in the back, a service area. We chatted about bikes and the different type of bicyclists - street versus off-road.

"It seems generational," said Vince. "The younger riders like mountain biking for the adrenaline rush - the X-game factor. Jumping over things. Every mountain biker I know has been to the hospital for some reason. But when you're 50 and 60, falling isn't what you want to do. Healing from injuries takes longer."

Every Sunday, Vince and a group of riders get together and go on rides to places like the Avenue of the Giants or the Tour of the Unknown Coast route. Between the Sunday rides and the rides to Life Cycle from his home in McKinleyville, Vince figures he clocks 150 miles a week in the winter, more in the summer. That's a lot of slices of pie he's burning!

I was curious how Vince got to be the pie baker in his household.

"My mother always baked," said Vince. "She told me I better learn how to cook because my future wife wouldn't be able to cook as good as her." So his Armenian mother showed him how to cook, and fortunately, he married a woman who also likes to cook.

Vince's mom thought pies should sit overnight and be served for breakfast. Vince remembered visiting her one time in 1971. When he got to her house he was starving, but his mom wouldn't let him eat the pie she had made, saying he could cut it in the morning. So Vince went to bed dreaming of pie for breakfast.

At 4 a.m. a big earthquake struck.

"The first thing my family wanted to know was if the pie was okay. When we checked the kitchen, the stove that the pie was on was in the middle of the kitchen. The pie had flopped onto the floor. That's when I wished I had eaten a slice the night before."

Baking pies grew out of the need to process apples from 50 apple trees in their former yard in Arcata. He could only make so much apple sauce.

"We got to know Kristi Wrigley's dad when he was running Wrigley's apple farm. He gave us some trees. Waltanas. Kings. I made the pies to use the apples. We had two kids in the house then and we could eat two pies a day."

It got so that Vince's pies became well known among his friends.

"One friend made a pottery pie plate that was this big around." He formed a big circle with his arms. "It took 20 medium apples to fill it."

Another friend wanted to one-up Vince by bringing a pie to a dinner party. She said she made it especially for Vince, the pie connoisseur, and was excited for him to taste it.

"When I took a bite, I was speechless," said Vince. "The pie was terrible. She was waiting for my response, so I asked her what type of apples were in her filling. They were like none I'd ever had before."

It turns out she had made a mock apple pie with Ritz crackers instead of apple slices.

"It was the worst apple pie!" said Lynn, adding that Vince's was the best.

"I just use Grandma Rose's recipe," said Vince with a shrug. And he only bakes apple pies when apples are in season.

Instead of water, Grandma Rose's pie crust recipe uses orange juice which gives the crust a tang and a slight orange tint. He brushes the top with egg wash - a beaten egg watered down - to give the crust a nice brown color. To make it flaky, he sticks the pie in the refrigerator for a couple of hours after he assembles it to give the crust a chance to relax and to solidify the shortening. Vince explained, and for the first time I understood, why you should use cold ingredients and not handle the crust too much.

The shortening, coated with flour, expands when it's heated and makes the dough flake up, like a pastry. When you handle the dough too much, you heat it up and the water in the shortening separates from the oil. You want the water to give a burst of steam when it's baking, and raise up the crust. It's simple science. When Vince is ready to bake his pie, he puts it straight from the fridge into a hot 350 degree oven to get that puffing effect.

I came back Monday to pick up an apple pie that he baked on his day off. It was still warm. Cinnamon wafted from its filling.

When Dan came home and saw the pie on the stove top, he declared, "Wow. That's a good-looking pie." And it was. The crust was an orange tint with a golden shine to it. It made a nice raised arc, and upon closer inspection, it was crackled looking, like distressed furniture.

We cut into it and plopped a scoop of vanilla ice cream on top. The apples were tart, perhaps a bit too tart for me. But the crust. Oh, the crust. It was everything I was searching for: color, flakiness, lightness and taste.

I didn't care if an earthquake struck tonight. I had tasted Vince's pie.

My Favorite Pie Crust

From "Grandma Rose's Book of Sinfully Delicious Cakes, Cookies, Pies, Cheese Cakes, Cake Rolls & Pastries" by Rose Naftalin, Random House, 1975. The book's out of print now, probably because the title was too long!

Makes two 9" crusts

2-1/2 c. all-purpose flour
1/2 tsp. salt
1/2 c. cold sweet butter
1/2 c. shortening
4 T. cold orange juice

Sift dry ingredients in bowl. Add butter and shortening. Rub with fingertips until it looks pebbly. You can work the dough at this point without fear of over handling. (Vince uses his Cuisinart to blend) At the next point be cautious: With a knife, cut orange juice into butter-flour mixture until it forms a ball. Roll out and line a pie pan.

Traditional Apple Pie

4 c. thinly sliced tart apples (about 5 large apples. Vince likes King or Gravenstein)
1/2 to 1 c. granulated sugar
2 tsp. cinnamon
1 egg for wash

Preheat oven to 400 degrees.
Peel, core and slice apples and toss with cinnamon and sugar. Layer apples in crust. Fold top crust around bottom crust and press a design around the rim with a fork or by hand. Right before it's ready to go in the oven, brush top with egg wash. Place pie on lower shelf of hot oven. After 15 minutes reduce heat to 350 degrees and continue baking for 35 additional minutes, or until juice bubbles (take care crust doesn't get too dark). Remove from oven and place on rack to cool.

An A+

Lincoln Elementary School principal gives Evelyn the thumbs up.

Every other year, Humboldt County hosts an Author Festival. About 25 children's book authors locally and from around the United States visit area schools to talk about what it's like to be an author. The schools do all kinds of projects to prepare for the visit, and the authors are treated like celebrities complete with their name posted on the school's outdoor message board.

I had the pleasure of visiting Lincoln Elementary School in Eureka, where Kim Emerson is the library technician. Every school library needs a person like Kim who is excited about books and enthusiastic about sharing them with kids. There's nothing worse than going to a school and finding out the librarian or teachers didn't read any of your books to their classes. The kids at Lincoln were on top of it. After fielding questions such as "How many books have you made?" "What's your favorite book?" and "How old are you?", Kim showed me what the kids had done to prepare for my visit. There was a door of frogs, a wall of bagels, and the tooth fairy with a cutout of my face on it. After the tour, I was invited to eat lunch in the teachers' room.

You never know what schools will dish up as food when you do these visits. I've gotten stuck with remnants of cafeteria food and store bought desserts that are so sugary that I wound up in a coma. Not Lincoln. They had great salads, yummy side dishes, and homemade desserts. I had a feeling I could mine a good pie baker from this group.

While signing books between bites, I mentioned to the teachers that I was working on a pie book.

"Evelyn makes great pies," everyone chimed. A quiet woman with stately posture paused mid-forkful as all attention turned to her. Like the shy kid in class who wishes she could disappear when she gets called on, Evelyn Smith meekly slipped me her phone number.

A few weeks later she invited me back to the teachers' room to meet. It was a place where she felt comfortably at home. That's because she has been working at Lincoln for the past 10 years as a sub-in for secretary, health aid, monitor, and literature tec. Prior to that she had worked for Alice Birney school for 24 years as an instructional aid and attendance clerk until she retired. But after her husband died, she came out of retirement to work at Lincoln.

"I missed the kids."

Evelyn's daughter, Shelly Smith, teaches a first and second grade combination class there. It had to be great having mom around, especially for potlucks at the school.

"Do you make pies, too?" I asked Shelly.

"Don't have to!" she said. Although in her classroom the kids make Thumpkin Pie right before Thanksgiving.

To make Thumpkin Pies, Shelly uses her mom's pie dough recipe and the recipe from the Libby's pumpkin can. The kids press the dough into a cupcake tin with their thumbs, spoon in some filling, then Shelly cooks the pies in a toaster oven for 45 minutes. Voila! Mini pumpkin pies they made themselves!

Today Evelyn brought three pies - raspberry with whipped cream topping, berry, and a coconut praline. As she put them out on the table decorated with a festive fall tablecloth, mumblings of "umms," "oh, good, she brought the coconut one," and "I'm going to have a slice of each" filled the room. The word must have gotten out, because the teachers' room was suddenly busy and even the principal who was on the Atkins diet stopped by. He insisted to the chiding teachers that pie was an acceptable Atkins food.

Evelyn, who grew up in the Weott area, learned how to make pie crusts from her husband. Her mother-in-law was a good baker, and passed that skill on to her son. Since then she's had lots of years to practice and perfect her own baking skills. She's had so many requests for her recipes that she put together her own cookbooks.

Evelyn's friends supply her with fresh berries - youngberry, logan berry, olallieberry, and boysenberry. The raspberries she was lucky to still find at the grocery store.

"I buy the berries from my friends, and fill my freezer up for the winter," said Evelyn. "Then for potlucks, I brings pies to share."

One of her crowd pleasers is the coconut praline pie. She got the recipe from Zola Oldridge and says it makes a good anytime pie. I love pralines and Dan loves coconut, so this one was sure to be a hit in our household.

A table full of awaiting teachers and I dug in. More sounds of jubilation encircled the room as we sampled each pie.

"We've gotten spoiled. We want our own flavors," commented Fran, the school's community liaison (and Evelyn's golf partner.)

I was definitely partial to the raspberry despite that the whipped cream had melted since the room was the temperature of a sauna, but the berry pie was also good. It was made out of olallieberries, which I'd never had before. They are much like blackberries. The one that was quite fantastic was the coconut praline. I'm not a coconut lover, but I can tolerate it when it's mixed with other delicious flavors, and this combination of nuts, pudding and Dream Whip did the trick. This pie would be a nice twist on the traditional pecan pie served at Thanksgiving dinner.

I'd give it an A+, or if I was in Shelly's classroom, two thumbs up!

Pastry for Two Pie Crusts

2 c. sifted flour
1 tsp. salt
2/3 c. plus 2 T. shortening
5 T. cold water

Mix flour and salt together. With pastry blender, cut in half the shortening until it looks like meal. Cut in the remaining shortening until particles are the size of giant peas. Sprinkle with the water, a tablespoon at a time, mixing lightly with a fork until the flour is moistened. Gather dough together so it cleans the bowl. Press into a ball, then roll out, or keep in waxed paper in the refrigerator until needed.

Coconut Praline Pie

1/2 c. chopped pecans or walnuts
1/3 c. butter
1/3 c. brown sugar
1 baked pie shell
2 packages Dream Whip
2-1/4 c. cold milk, divided into 1 and 1-1/4 cups
1 tsp. vanilla
2 packages vanilla instant pudding
1-1/3 c. shredded coconut

Heat pecans, butter and brown sugar in pan until butter and sugar are melted and mixture comes to a boil. Boil exactly 30 seconds. Remove from heat and spread on bottom of baked pie shell. Let cool. Beat Dream Whip, 1 cup milk and vanilla on high speed about 6 minutes or until thick. Add remaining 1-1/4 cup milk and pudding mixes, blend on low speed, beat on high for 2 minutes. Stir in 1 cup coconut. Spoon into pie shell. Refrigerate at least 4 hours or until set. Garnish with remaining coconut.

Apple Pie of My Eye

Kristi Wrigley picks apples at Wrigleys' Apples.

I am fortunate to live in an area that has apple orchards, each with their own specialties: Clendenen's Cider Works, Arrington Apples, Wrigleys' Apples, and Fieldbrook Valley Apple Farms. During the Fortuna Apple Harvest Festival, Clendenen's is a main attraction, giving tractor tours of their orchards. C.E. Clendenen purchased the orchard about 100 years ago in 1905, and it has been passed down through the generations. They make cider on an old rack-and-cloth press.

Arrington Apples is popular with people getting married. Dan and I went to a wedding there one sunny September afternoon, and it was magical. Trees drooped with Eureka Red Kings the size of both of my fists put together. There was an Adam and Eve feeling in the air as little kids plucked apples off trees despite signs forbidding guests not to.

A trip to Wrigley's makes for a beautiful Sunday drive, plus it has my favorite apple - Waltanas.

Two years ago I went to Fieldbrook Valley Apple Farms's Apple Festival. Fieldbrook Valley Apple Farm on Rock Pit Road was started by Betty and Dick Lovie as a retirement project. It now produces over 50 varieties of apples.

When I pulled into the farm I was directed by a gangly teenage boy to park in a grassy field. I moseyed about the little set up that hark back to small-town festivals from the '30s. There were tables covered with apple pies ready for judging. Folks sitting around tables eating pie with vanilla ice cream. A couple of craft booths with local knickknacks. And an enclosure with an open front where baskets of apples lined the walls. The apples were arranged from sweet to tart and a friendly worker took his time slicing off a green, red or yellow crescent of a freshly-picked apple so that people could sample the flavors and choose which apples they wanted to buy.

I found that I preferred more tart apples with a firm texture. Some apples I wanted strictly for eating, so I dropped a few in my bag.

Others I wanted for making an apple pie.

"Which apples make the best apple pie?" I asked one female worker, busy ringing up a customer.

"Depending on what kind of flavor you want. Some people like the apples to be soft so they almost turn to apple sauce. Others want firm apples to hold their shape. Some people like tart apples. Others sweet."

Mushy was out. Firm was good, but not too firm that you'd have trouble cutting them with a fork. A hint of tartness to cut the sweetness of the white sugar was best.

The worker finished up with her customer and then stepped out from behind the cash register where rows of dipped caramel apples lined up like paratroopers waiting for the command to jump. She glanced over at the pies submitted into the pie tasting contest and lowered her voice as if imparting a secret.

"The best apple pies I ever make are when I mix my apples. That way you get some firmness and some softness, and the tart and sweet blend together. That's my advice."

A sigh of relief. Now I wouldn't have to fret about choosing the perfect apple. I randomly went from basket to basket and took one of these, two of those, and another of that until I had a paper bag bulging with fresh-picked apples of all kinds.

I bought a caramel apple with nuts for the ride home, and that afternoon, made a mixed apple pie. It was one of the best ever, receiving the Husband Stamp of Approval.

But the best apple pie I ever baked was made entirely with Waltanas from Wrigleys' Apples which I brought to Thanksgiving dinner to share with Dan's family in Portland, Oregon. It was so perfect in color, taste, texture and tradition that I even I was surprised at how well it turned out.

Here are some tips from the apple experts, and a listing of where you can get many varieties of apples locally.

Tips from Janet Arrington of Arrington Apples:
* Use cake flour or pastry flour for the pie dough. It's finer and makes a delicate and tender crust, though not as flaky.
* Use brown and white sugar mixed rather than just white.
* Instead of only Crisco, combine butter, shortening and lard for better flavor and crispiness.

* Add a little sour cream when mixing your apples for the filling. Just a coating will do.
* If your apples are too sweet, too tart, or old, add a pinch of salt to bring out the flavor.
* Use apples that are in season.
* Use Mexican vanilla.

Janet's apple recommendations:
* The Jonagolds make the best apple pies
* Gravensteins also make a "hell of a pie" because they are tart and sweet
* She also likes Waltanas
* She says the "old timers" prefer Bellflower because it's tart and holds its shape.

Clif Clendenen's recommendations:
* Try a mixed pie with Idared and Bellflower apples
* Blushing Goldens are more tart and stay firm when cooked
* Use sweet Golden Delicious when making sugar-free pies

Where to Buy Local Pie Apples

Arrington Apples, Eureka
Jonagold, Golden Delicious, Gravenstein, Waltanas, Bellflower

Clendenen's Cider Works, Fortuna
Mutsu, Idared, Jonagold, Golden Delicious, Esopus Spitzenberg (Thomas Jefferson's favorite apple), Gravenstein, Pippin, Granny Smith, Blushing Golden, Bellflower

Fieldbrook Valley Apple Farms, Fieldbrook
50+ varieties including Macintosh, Braeburn, Honeycrisp, Cameo, Rubinstar Jonagold, Red Rome, Pippin, Mutsu Crispin, Fuji, Gala, Gravenstein, Jonagold, Spartan, Lustre Elstar, Empire, Carousel

Wrigleys' Apples, South Eureka
Gravensteins, Mellon (Late Gravensteins), Kings, Waltanas

Dump and Pour

Kristi dumps sugar in a bowl without measuring.

To get to Wrigleys' Apples you have to go south of Eureka out on Elk River Road, past two covered bridges to Wrigley Road, then follow the signs which lead you through a redwood forest.

Wrigleys' Apples orchards have been in the family for 100 years. George E. Wrigley, bought the orchard in 1903. His son, Irving, inherited it in 1928. The current owner, Kristi Wrigley, inherited the property from Irving, her father. She's concerned about what will be left to pass on.

Sadly, the fruit production of her apple trees has dramatically decreased. The orchard sits near a river that captures runoff from land that has been "overlogged." The water table has risen, rotting the roots of the trees, and flood levels have gotten higher and higher, only to recede and leave a choking top layer that doesn't allow enough oxygen to the roots.

"My trees are stressed and may eventually die," said Kristi who has been fighting to save her orchards for seven years. "They certainly aren't producing apples like they used to."

One variety being affected is the Waltanas. Waltanas were introduced to the Wrigley family by Kristi's uncle Ted, a dentist who had patients in Southern Humboldt where the apple was developed.

Waltanas are a hybrid apple that was developed by the Etter family, or who Kristi refers to as the "Luther Burbanks of Humboldt County." She surmises that it is a cross between four apples. "I'm pretty sure it's Wagner. I think there's some King. I know there's crabapple. And there's one mystery apple that I haven't figured out yet."

Waltanas are a late harvest apple that are ready for picking in the latter part of October through November and keep well into February. She says it is one of the few apples that reaches its prime after it is picked, and has a three-month shelf life. It is dense and hard like a crabapple, but has a cream-colored flesh. And boy howdy - it's tasty!

"It's the best apple because it comes into season during the height of pie baking, from Thanksgiving to Christmas," said Kristi. "Those who like eating apples say Waltanas are the best, and those who like baking apples say Waltanas are the best. I agree with both."

The much anticipated Waltanas were ready the weekend of Nov. 15 and 16, so I drove down on Sunday to get my box of apples. When I drove up to the gate a sign saying "No more Waltanas" was posted. Drat! I missed them. As I stewed in the car about why I hadn't driven down there on a Saturday instead, one, two, then three cars pulled up behind me. An older gentleman got out, read the sign, and said, "I was looking forward to getting those apples. Maybe next year."

Or maybe not. Kristi got less than 200 boxes of Waltanas from this year's crop - the least since she's been picking.

"I should get two boxes minimum per tree. I have 500 Waltana trees and used to get over 1,000 boxes. You can't tell me my trees aren't affected."

In 1994-95 season, Kristi and her dad sold Waltanas into February. Shortly after, her father died. That same year the orchard flooded six times. The next year there were only 750 boxes. After being flooded more times after that - more than she can remember during her lifetime of growing up there - coupled with her experience as a surveyor at Caltrans, she put it together that logging was causing the flooding which was choking her trees.

"Not only do I have trees with mud up to here," she held her hand hip high, "but the mud is burying my fences so animals just walk right in and help themselves to my fruit." Just the other day a bear got into the shed and ate a 25 pound box of apples.

Even though I wasn't able to get any Waltanas, I was lucky enough to have Kristi bake me an apple pie with the ones that she kept for herself. Here it was mid-December and the apples were still juicy.

"They keep three to six months," said Kristi. "That's why we planted them. So people can still eat fresh, local apples in Decembber."

Although Kristi admitted to being better known for her pumpkin pie and yeast breads, at Thanksgiving and Christmas she makes apple pies. Kristi learned from her mom and Auntie Ruth Braghetta how to bake.

"It was the dump and pour method. There's no recipe. We can make bread or yeast dough blindfolded. If we didn't have milk, we used water or apple juice. You can tell by the consistency when it's ready."

She darted her brown eyes at me. "Makes people mad when you tell them you don't have a recipe."

Kristi chucked another log in the French range situated in her country kitchen. The heat seeped into my bones.

"The range is from my mother's old house. It's what you used to see in lumber camps. The top gets hot and they'd cook up a big batch of pancakes."

Kristi got out the ingredients for her pie dough which would be enough to make two pies. "If you're going to make a pie, you might as well make two."

She poured in about 4 cups of unbleached flour ("unbleached is not as stiff and angry to roll out"), Crisco shortening, white vinegar and ice water. Then, with a special fork, she pushed the flour to the back side of the bowl, scooped a little toward her, added a few tablespoons of the water mixture, and worked it around with the fork until it stuck together. Then she put the dough onto a sheet of cellophane wrap and, using the wrap, pushed it together to make a ball. She repeated the process until she had one big ball which she squashed flat and put in the refrigerator.

Next she sliced up her apples, some the size of grapefruits.

"Pies are not about the crust or the topping. It's the apples you use in the filling, and the love that comes out of your heart and through your hands."

She sprayed the bottom of her tin with oil "so the crust doesn't stick when you try to get it out," rolled out a bottom crust in the wrap, dumped some apples in to cover the bottom crust, sprinkled on some sugar and cinnamon, then added another layer which she sprinkled again. Kristi doesn't use any thickener like flour or corn-

217

starch, and if the apples are a little old and not so juicy, she adds a few tablespoons of water. A nice mound of filling awaited the topping.

"My kids like the apple crisp topping instead of a crust."

Again, Kristi dumped and poured some sugar and flour and tamped it on the top of the mound. Then into the oven it went.

While the pies cooked, we warmed our aching backs against the range. She talked about what she would do if she could just work the orchards, and not have to have another job as well. "If I had the time, I'd make apple cider vinegar. And I'd like to make recipe books with apple recipes, you know, things I can market with the apples."

She shook her head. "It saddens me when I can't carry on traditions. It's not about the money. It's about the daughter who brought her grandmother back to the apple farm so she could see where she used to come as a child. It's about people who come back here every year to get apples for Thanksgiving."

Crisp Topping

1 heaping c. of flour
1 scant c. of sugar
1 cube (1/2 c.) of butter ("I do mean butter. Preferably Challenge.")

Cut butter into flour/sugar mixture until crumbly. Pat onto top of apples in pie crust. Bake 10 minutes at 400 degrees. Turn down to 350 degrees; bake until apples are tender and soft.

Here's another topping, measured out, that can be put on the last 15 minutes of baking.

Brown Sugar Topping

1/3 c. all-purpose flour
1/3 c. packed brown sugar
2 T. butter
1/4 tsp. ground cinnamon
1/8 tsp. ground cloves

Mix all ingredients until crumbly. Sprinkle over pie.

The Mother of All Pie Days

My pies almost caused a rebellion at the Lazutin household.

This was an exciting Thanksgiving in Arizona for my mom since all her kids would be visiting. It doesn't happen often that the whole brood can make family gatherings. So when we do, it's a big deal.

Mom had the main meal plus a pumpkin cheesecake covered. I was to be the official pie maker. She figured with all the knowledge I had gathered and pies I had tasted, that I could whip up some show stoppers.

Pecan and Sugarless Apple Pie were my recipes of choice, the sugarless one because my parents are diabetic and I didn't want my pies to send them into a sugar coma.

Trying to be the organized daughter, I sent ahead recipes via email so that I wouldn't forget to pack them. Mom, being the organized mother, printed them out and fetched the ingredients.

Tra-la-la.

For two nights and one day before Thanksgiving the family was on the go trying a new sushi restaurant in Scottsdale, watching Ron and Nina's videos of their cruise in Germany and renovations of their new apartment, having a combined birthday party for the October and November birthday people, and taking walks around the man-made lake behind my parents' house to see the golf cart that someone had driven into the lake. There was no time to make pies. Tomorrow, I kept telling myself. There's always tomorrow.

Well, Thanksgiving morning rolled around and it was now or never. I decided to make an additional pecan pie since we were going to visit Dan's dad later that day and he loves pecan pie.

Using Sylvia's recipe for four pie crusts, I measured out the flour. I opened the pantry door and looked for the shortening.

"Mom? Where's the Crisco?"

"There's Wesson oil."

"Oil?"

"That's what I use to make my crusts."

Oh, no. That sinking feeling of impending doom slithered into my gut.

"But I don't know if this recipe will work with oil."

"Here," she said, pouring oil into the flour, "It's a no-fail crust."

"But that's not the point, Mom. I'm supposed to be the pie maker so that you don't have to be."

With nine hungry people doing nothing more than waiting for dinner to be served, pressure was on and timing was everything. She couldn't afford to have my pies delay her side dishes. She poured more oil in the bowl and stirred vigorously. I turned my attention to the fillings. I decided to make the pecan ones first so I stirred all the ingredients but the nuts together.

"Mom? Where's the pecans?"

By this time she was wrestling with the crust, squishing it between waxed paper.

"In the bag on the right."

There was a plastic bag of measured out chopped pecans - for one pie. That was my fault I sprung two pecan pies on her last minute. But there should be plenty of pecans to make another pie.

"Where's the rest of the bag?"

"The nuts are on the shelf."

Oh no. Must...resist...sinking...feeling...

My mom didn't buy the pecans you can get in the baking section that are already shelled. She bought these nuts from the corner fruit stand. Granted they were fresh, but they weren't cracked. I kept the irony that we were having canned yams for dinner, but freshly cracked pecan pie for dessert under wraps.

We put a team of nutcrackers to work and about 30 minutes later, I had enough for both fillings. In the meantime, I sliced apples and Mom struggled with rolling out the dough. "It's not rolling out," she mumbled. "It's supposed to be no-fail."

She managed to get three oily slabs of dough rolled out enough to fit into three pie tins. I poured pecan filling in two of them then rushed them to the oven.

Luckily she has two ovens, well, really one since the turkey took up all of the other. I started on the sugarless apple pie, boiling the sliced apples in the apple juice concentrate until they were translucent. Once seasoned with cinnamon, I dumped the apple filling in the remaining pie tin. Then trouble. There wasn't enough dough to make a top crust. If I was thinking fast on my feet, I would have made Kristi Wrigley's Crisp Topping. But wait a minute! This was supposed to be a sugarless apple pie! Mom rolled out an amoebic blob from the remaining dough and plunked it on top. A wide rim of apples still showed. I fretted. It was ugly.

"That's okay," said my Mom. "Get it in the oven."

Miraculously the pies were done in time for the side dishes to heat. The pecan pies looked normal, but the exposed apples got burnt. My heart sank. The sugarless apple pie was supposed to be my pride and joy - the pie that could save everyone from going over the dessert deep end after the most caloric dinner of the year.

Dinner was fabulous, yadda-yadda. The stuffing with sausage was a hit. Then it was time for dessert. Fortunately, Mom had made a pumpkin cheesecake, so I went for that. Dan went for pecan, his favorite. Some of the other brave souls went for the apple, but hedged their bets with slices of pecan and pumpkin as well.

None of my family will admit it, but my pies were bad. The crust didn't taste good, nor did it act like crust. It kinda crumbled like wet sand. The burnt apples were yucky. So what should have been a glorious presentation of the cream de la desserts, turned out to be something I wish I could have accidentally dropped in the trash.

My mom always says I'm too hard on myself. Nobody died (or went into a coma) from the intake of my pies that day, so I guess I should be happy. And being one to look for the good stuff in bad situations, here are some tips I learned that I'll pass along to avoid a Thanksgiving disaster.

1. Don't assume everyone knows what Crisco is. Write "Crisco shortening" instead.

2. If you're cooking in someone else's kitchen, check to see that they have the ingredients and tools (pie tins, measuring spoons, etc.) that you need.

3. Don't wait until Thanksgiving morning to make your pies. Make them the day before. Not everyone has two ovens.

4. Don't make more pies than you planned to unless you checked ahead and verified that there was enough ingredients.

5. Use store-bought shelled nuts. It's easier and they taste just as good.

6. No-fail crusts can fail. Have backup ingredients. (Looking back on her recipe, I realized she didn't use the cold milk, just the oil, and I had four cups of flour instead of her usual two.)

7. Above all else remember, a pie made from scratch is still better than a store-bought one if only because your family appreciates the effort you made.

In my opinion, if you're going to eat dessert, go all the way! Use real butter, sugar and fat! Like Marge Taylor says, "Thanksgiving is no time to cut back." But for all of you who still have the slightest bit of guilt about eating pie, or have diabetes, here's a sugarless apple pie recipe. It's surprisingly good. The recipe is from the Blue Lake Museum Cookbook submitted by Nicole Barker.

No Sugar Sweet Apple Pie

6 c. sweet apples
1 12 oz. can frozen apple juice
2 T. tapioca
1 tsp. cinnamon

Slice apples for pie. Cook over stove with apple juice and tapioca until transparent to bring natural sweetener out. Add cinnamon. Make pastry for 2 crust pie. Add filling and dot with butter. Bake at 425 degrees for 50 to 60 minutes.

Author's Note: Let filling cool before pouring into pastry.

How could I mention Thanksgiving without including the mother of all Thanksgiving pies - pumpkin pie?

Pumpkin Pie

One 9" pie crust
2 eggs
3/4 c. sugar
1 16 oz. can of pumpkin
1 12 oz. can evaporated milk
1 tsp. ground cinnamon
1/2 tsp. salt
1/2 tsp. ground ginger
1/4 tsp. ground cloves

Prepare pastry. Heat oven to 425 degrees. Beat eggs slightly with hand beater. Beat in remaining ingredients. To alleviate spilling, place pastry-lined pie plate on oven rack and pour in filling. Bake 15 minutes.

Reduce oven temperature to 350 degrees. Bake until knife inserted in center comes out clean, about 45 minutes. Refrigerate until chilled, about 4 hours. Top with whipped cream.

Sweet Endings

Seconds anyone?

After my Thanksgiving Day disaster, I found myself reaching for ready-made pie crusts in the frozen food section. Just before I'd put them in my cart, a voice in my head would say, "How could you let a little flour, shortening, salt and water defeat you? Buck up!" I threw the crusts back on the shelf like they were frozen Frisbees.

Being under the spotlight puts a lot of pressure on people. When an ordinary task turns into a production witnessed by an audience suddenly meringues fail, crusts burn, and fruit doesn't ripen.

I talked to John Bush months after our pecan pie night fiasco, and he said, "I made a great pecan pie the other day. No one was around. There was no pressure, and everything worked out beautifully."

Set aside your pressures, and simply enjoy the process of creating a treat that brings a smile to people's faces. And don't let one bad experience deter you from making a pie from scratch. Just remember, vanilla ice cream or whipped cream can cover up most mistakes.

Besides, no matter what ingredients you use to make it special - be it apple cider vinegar, brown sugar or egg wash - the best pies are made with love and taste even better when shared with a friend.

How To Order More Books

For additional copies of this cookbook, return this order form and a
check or money order made out to **Natasha Wing** to:

Wing Books
75 Sunkist Lane
Arcata, CA 95519-9274

_ _

Please send me _____ copies of "A Slice of Humboldt Pie" at
$15.00 per copy plus $3.00 for shipping and handling per book.

Enclosed is my payment for $_____.

Mail my books to:

Name_____
Address_____
City_____State_____Zip_____

_ _

Please send me _____ copies of "A Slice of Humboldt Pie" at
$15.00 per copy plus $3.00 for shipping and handling per book.

Enclosed is my payment for $_____.

Mail my books to:

Name_____
Address_____
City_____State_____Zip_____